HEALTHY MEAL PREP:

THE ULTIMATE BEGINNERS GUIDE WITH DELICIOUS RECIPES FOR A 3 WEEKS MEAL PLAN TO HEAL THE IMMUNE SYSTEM LOSE WEIGHT AND IMPROVING YOUR HEALTH

By Emma Lopez

Table of Contents

9

Chapter 1: Why Healthy Meal Prep?

Eating healthy and maintaining a balanced diet is the basis for developing a practical and well-organized meal plan. This process begins with learning about healthy food choices, making wise selections for everyday use and meal planning, then creating a schedule that works best to improve your lifestyle. Meal prep is important because it sets the foundation for better, well-thought-out choices for recipes and ideas for breakfast, lunch, dinner, and snacks. Once you know which foods to include, and a plan to work with, preparation becomes easier and routine. A new, refreshing way of eating will become effortless over time, with a delicious menu to enjoy each day.

1.1 Eating Healthier

A healthy diet is one of the most important investments you'll make in life. It requires understanding the basics of nutrition and changing bad habits you may not consider problematic. There are a lot of myths about which types of food are healthy, including debates on low carb and ketogenic diets, whether or not a restrictive meal plan is sustainable and concerns about the long-term effects of low-calorie diets. In general, all diets have some merit, though most people who eagerly begin a new way of eating often grow bored and often quit. Other people may continue longer, only to become dissatisfied with the results, expecting overnight changes.

The Importance of Choosing Healthy Foods

Eating healthy is important in keeping our body, mind, and lifestyle well balanced and in good function. Developing bad habits can be reversed when you try new, tasty foods that you may not have considered before. Often, there is the false perception that healthy foods are less delicious and flavorful as their processed or packaged counterparts, which is untrue. In fact, natural foods have a variety of distinct flavors, textures, and uses that can fit into any lifestyle, preference, and budget.

Why is it important to choose to eat healthily? Your well being depends on it! Eating well gives you the power to prevent disease and improve the way you feel and function in life. People with a healthy diet have more energy, a positive outlook, and generally feel better. If you feel better, you'll likely have a better outlook on life, and want to continue eating and living healthy for its effects. The biggest challenge most people face is changing bad habits and switching from processed, high sugar, and sodium products to natural, wholesome foods with no packaging or additives. Depending on how you currently eat, this may be a major overhaul or require some minor changes. Either way, there are steps everyone can take towards adapting to a healthy, sustainable diet for life.

The Benefits of Healthy Eating

Healthy eating provides numerous benefits once you make the switch to consuming wholesome, natural foods. You'll notice some positive effects right away, while other benefits occur over time. It's important to maintain consistency when making changes to get the most out of your healthy way of eating. Most people expect or want changes immediately, and for this reason, some people become easily discouraged and slip back into their previous habits of consuming unhealthy, processed foods. It's best to make the commitment for the long run and focus on milestones and goals along the way. Consider the goal of eating better as a lifelong adventure into eating better for you.

What are the benefits of healthy eating, and when do they take effect? While it's necessary to view changes to your diet as long-term, there are some good results you'll notice in the early stages of your new diet. These are just the beginning of a new way of eating, and should inspire you to continue:

- *Digestion improves within the first week.* Fruits and vegetables are easily processed by the body, and their nutrients transported through the bloodstream. Enzymes play a key role in absorbing and using nutrients in raw foods. Cutting down and eliminating processed foods means your body will have less of a challenge in breaking everything to use and producing waste. If you experienced any stomach cramps or indigestion before, you might find some relief during the first few days or weeks.

- *Insulin levels become balanced.* If you currently have high blood sugar and/or are at risk or in the early stages of pre-diabetes, eating natural foods will reduce the spikes in sugar and create a more level, balanced insulin levels. Natural foods contain just the right amount of sugar, which is natural and unprocessed so that your body can easily break them down and use it for energy. Always avoid refined forms of sugars, which include corn syrup with unnaturally high levels of fructose, along with other artificial options, and you'll notice a significant difference in glucose in a short period of time.

- **Mood levels will stabilize, and you'll feel better**. For some people, high amounts of refined sugar, food coloring, and processed foods have a mood-altering effect, and can also impact their cognitive function. The destabilized swing of sugar levels alone can cause a rapid change in mood and behavior as a result. Once you choose natural sources of food to replace artificial options, you'll notice a stable sense of feeling well, as opposed to significant changes in the way you feel and react. Studies on children with Attention Deficit Disorder and various anxiety conditions have shown significant improvement by eliminating processed foods and replacing them with fresh fruits and foods without refined ingredients. This change in diet has also benefited adults with depression and anxiety, as well.

- ***Loss of Excessive Weight.*** If your goal is to lose excess weight, you'll be pleasantly surprised by the impact of eating better within the first two weeks. For some people, weight loss may occur quickly, which may decrease or plateau, while other people see gradual changes over time, resulting in a significant loss within several months. Since everybody size and type is different, it's difficult to determine the exact results, though a major change in diet, coupled with an active lifestyle, can increase the amount of weight loss in the early stages of eating and living better.

Once you become settled into a new way of eating well and experience the early benefits of these positive changes, you may want to learn more about the impact of long-term advantages and how a wholesome meal plan can create a better outcome for your health over a period of months and years:

- **Prevention of Disease.** Centuries of research indicate a significant shift in the prevention and treatment of chronic conditions and disease as a result of eating a balanced, healthy diet. For example, a diet low in trans fats and processed foods results in a lower risk of developing cancer and heart disease. Healthy fats, as found in natural oils and avocado, can improve heart and cardiovascular health, while deep-fried, fatty foods containing trans fats promote the growth of free radicals, which can lead to the accelerating of mutated cells, resulting in cancerous tumors. Long term conditions, such as type 1 and 2 diabetes, and high glucose levels, are far more manageable on a balanced, wholesome diet.

- **Improved Management of Chronic Conditions.** Arthritis, fibromyalgia, and other chronic conditions often cause ongoing pain and discomfort, which negatively impact the quality of life for people who suffer from these conditions. Eating a well-balanced diet can effectively reduce or eliminate inflammation, which significantly reduces pain. Weight loss, for chronic sufferers who are obese, will also experience comfort from weight loss and the reduction in inflammation. The loss of weight relieves the pressure off of bones, joints, and nerves, which also reduces pain.

- *Long-Term Weight Management.* Losing weight is one major goal, and keeping it off can be another challenge. Maintaining a consistently healthy way of eating will ensure that your weight will always be manageable, long after you shed the unwanted pounds. Most people find that after losing a lot of weight, in cases where they are considered obese, there is a time period where the process will plateau or slow down. At this point, you may have already reached your goal weight, or you can choose to make additional enhancements to the way you eat and exercise, to slim down more. In general, eating a healthy diet will maintain your weight within a reasonable range, so that you can adjust your goals according to your personal ideals.

- *More Energy and Endurance.* Initially, and in the long term, you'll notice a higher level of energy that is very different than the sugar "rush" or a sudden, temporary spike in energy that results from an energy drink or snack. Natural sources of protein, vitamins, and fiber will not only give you a better source of energy, but you'll also have more endurance and strength as well. This is ideal for exercise and high-impact activities, such as marathons, swimming, and daily jogging. In daily life, you'll have more energy to handle more errands and function better at work and in general.

- *A Better Outlook on Life.* Once your mind and body adjust to a better way of living and eating, and you experience many (if not all) of the positive effects, it will greatly change your outlook on life. People with chronic conditions and pain will notice less inflammation and better mobility. Mood and behavior will become balanced due to regular nutrients to support the brain and cognitive performance. Depression and anxiety are often reduced as well. Overall, many of the benefits on the physical body and mental well-being have a positive result on the psychological health too.

1.2 Saving Money and Time

One of the most significant challenges to eating well is making it work within a budget and allowing for enough time for planning ahead. Most people have little or no time within their daily schedule to get everything done, not including meal planning and preparation for days or a week in advance. For this reason, it's important to find ways to reduce the time and effort needed to prepare and plan your meals, to avoid making the mistake of slipping into packaged and processed foods, instead of using natural foods and ingredients.

Choosing Healthy Foods That Fit Within Your Budget

The cost of food and eating well increases each year, though with careful planning and exploring new options. There are many ways to enjoy a healthy diet on a budget. Often, prices vary from one store or market to another and choosing quality while keeping the cost of your grocery bill down can be a challenge. Consider the following options when preparing for your next trip to the supermarket:

- **Research and visit local farmer's markets.**
  Some local markets may specialize in certain
  items, while others are widespread and feature
  many local farmers, artisans, and products. In
  some cases, shopping later in the afternoon may
  provide the opportunity for discounts on certain
  products, just before the market closes. Local
  produce, when in season, may be less expensive
  and offer more selection. When you shop local,
  you're getting a fresher product, because the
  product doesn't have to travel as far, which
  results in better quality.

- **Bulk shopping is ideal for your grains,
  beans, and baking ingredients.** Nuts, seeds,
  and dried fruits are also common in the bulk
  section of a store and make an excellent snack in
  place of chips, candy bars, and unhealthy
  options. One of the biggest advantages of buying
  in bulk is portion control, and the ability to buy
  only as much as you need. This will also keep the
  cost down and within a manageable level. If you
  need cashews or pistachios, for example,
  purchasing them in a large bag or container will
  be more expensive than in bulk, because you can

choose the exact portion and avoid paying for the cost of excess packaging.

- **Order from a local butcher.** If the option is available, split a large order between family or friends. This will ensure that you're getting the best quality of meat for your diet: local, naturally fed and raised. The larger order will last longer and provide more food to everyone sharing the order.

- **Invest in a freezer.** A small or medium-sized freezer for an apartment or a large deep freezer is an ideal investment for storing prepared meals that can last for weeks or months. This is a great way to store large amounts of food, packaged into smaller, serving-size portions for one or more people. A freezer will allow you to prepare and plan meals at least one week in advance. It's also an ideal method of turning home-cooked food into ready-made dinners, which are healthier, and familiar to your diet.

- **Prepare in advance and cook or bake in large amounts.** The bigger the batch of food, the less expensive it becomes during the week to enjoy smaller portions. Some food items or "super" size cartons or boxes of food can be less expensive and reduce the costs of shopping in the long term. If you shop at a large retailer or store that provides large cartons of certain items, this can be of benefit for families or groups of people splitting foods for meal preparation. These can be divided into smaller portions, and significantly reduce the costs of frequently used foods, such as canned fish, dried beans, frozen seafood, and large quantities or cartons of fruits and vegetables.

Easy Ingredients to Create Quick Recipes

Keeping an easy list of ingredients to buy and maintain on hand will provide a strong foundation for creating an easy-to-follow shopping list and compiling other foods to fit into your daily and weekly meal preparation. Most of these ingredients are basic, and will likely be a regular in the freezer, refrigerator, cupboard or pantry:

- *Frozen or Fresh Berries.* In season, berries are ideal fresh and can be enjoyed as a snack on their own, or in a bowl of milk (non-dairy or low-fat dairy milk) or natural yogurt. Frozen berries make a great addition to smoothies, along with banana and other fruits. When they are no longer in season, it's best to buy berries frozen; they are often available in various mixed varieties, or individually. Grocery stores tend to carry them year-round, which makes them easy to find, and keep on hand on a regular basis.

- **Whole grains.** In their whole, unrefined state, oats, barley, quinoa, millet, and other grains are an essential part of a healthy diet. They are high in fiber, protein, and provide a lot of energy in a small dose. Just one small bowl of hot oatmeal in the morning can provide hours of energy throughout the day. They are easily found in bulk stores, natural food stores, and grocers. The key to buying grains is to find organic, whole sources, and avoid flavored or sweetened pre-packaged options, which are often found in the same aisles or sections of the grocery store. If you prefer several different grains in your pantry, invest in several glass jars with secured lids for storage. Grains have a long shelf life, though it's best to use them up within a few months to enjoy them in their freshest state.

- **Natural sweeteners.** One of the key changes to improving your diet is cutting out sugar and refined, artificial sweeteners. Many boxed bowls of cereal and baked goods contain high fructose corn syrup, which is responsible for increasing weight gain and high glucose levels, even in small amounts. Keeping a few natural sweeteners on hand is a good way to curb a habit of eating refined sugar. Natural honey and maple syrup are good options to use in moderation. Low carb sweeteners, such as monk fruit, swerve, and erythritol, are also excellent, especially for maintaining healthy sugar levels.

- **Lean Meats.** Chicken, turkey, and seafood are excellent sources of lean meats to store in your freezer or refrigerator. For best quality, purchase your cuts of meat from a local butcher. If you choose to eat red meat, do so in moderation, and choose only lean (or extra lean) versions of beef and pork. Avoid smoked meats, processed sliced meats, and bacon, as they all contain numerous chemicals and additives that defeat the purpose of healthy eating.

- **Soy-based Foods.** If you are vegetarian, vegan, or looking to increase the amount of soy in your diet, it's a good idea to keep a small or moderate amount of soy products in your kitchen. Before you decide to include soy in your diet, it's important to determine which variety of soy you are most likely to consume often and keep this as a "go-to" option. Tofu, tempeh, miso, and edamame beans are popular choices and often found in most grocery stores and markets. Many soy products are reasonably priced, though you may want to consider organic or naturally grown soybean foods and products as your primary options. If you are new to soy, consider purchasing miso soup or paste to create a simple broth. Miso paste will generally last in the refrigerator for up to two weeks, while dried miso soup powder can be stored in the cupboard or pantry for several months. Edamame beans make a tasty snack with a light sprinkling of sea salt or pink Himalayan salt and are often found frozen.

- **Frozen and Fresh Vegetables.** It's ideal to keep a few varieties of frozen and/or fresh vegetables on hand for side dishes, casseroles, and other meals. Dark green vegetables contain the highest levels of calcium, protein, and fiber, and make a great addition to any meal of the day. Frozen spinach is usually available and sectioned into small, pre-cooked sections, making it easy to add to an omelet or scrambled eggs, or in a stew or soup. Broccoli and cauliflower make a great ingredient in casseroles, skillet meals, and soups. They can also be enjoyed raw as part of a vegetable platter. Canned olives, fresh mushrooms, carrots, celery, green peppers, are among many other options you can choose from in the produce section. Choose your favorite vegetables, and if you typically don't eat them, make a point of trying at least one or two new options each week. Kale, cabbage, bok choy, and root vegetables, such as yams, potatoes, squash, and turnips, are also great options to include in your recipes.

- **Nuts and Seeds.** If you are prone to snacking and need some healthy options in your kitchen or pantry, choose an assortment of nuts and seeds for this purpose. Peanuts, almonds, cashews, pecans, walnuts, and hazelnuts are all good sources of healthy fats, protein, and fiber. Pumpkin and sunflower seeds are also great options and can easily replace potato chips and candy as a better choice for snacking at home or on the go. Nuts and seeds are best unsalted and raw for nutritional value, though some lightly roasted peanuts or almonds make good options.

In general, when you choose the foods that become the staples or foundation of your new diet, make sure you are using them often so that you can plan your meals and preparation well in advance.

Building a Pantry

Creating an inventory of nutritious dry foods is the best foundation for a healthy meal plan. A pantry doesn't need to be complex or contain every single spice, herb, grain, and dried well either, just the items you prefer and decide to use in your recipes. It's important to evaluate the variety and types of items you wish to include, and keep a regular inventory of them, to prevent buying the same food twice or in excess.

- **Beans and legumes.** A few varieties of beans, lentils, chickpeas, and other dried or canned legumes are good to have on hand when preparing stews, soups, and dips. They are excellent sources of fiber and protein and can be easily added to a variety of meals to boost the nutrient level. Canned beans are great to have on hand in a pinch, while dried foods are excellent for longer-term use, allowing for more custom portions and sizing, depending on the recipe or meal. Chickpeas and lentils are good ingredients for stews and dips, such as hummus, as well as a protein boost in salads.

- **Whole Grains**. Quinoa, barley, oats, and wild and brown rice are among the top grains to include in your pantry. Quinoa is especially recommended for its high protein content (twice the amount of most grains), vitamins, and fiber.

- **Dried Fruits**. Raisins, dried berries (cranberries, cherries, blueberries, etc.), prunes, and apricots make excellent natural sources of sugar and sweeteners for recipes or as a snack on their own. Prunes are high in fiber and can be added to desserts as natural sugar. Dried berries and raisins make excellent ingredients in a trail mix or homemade granola. In a pinch, they can top a bowl of plain, natural yogurt or bowl of oatmeal.

- **Nuts, seeds, and mixed options**. All types of nuts make great snacks and ingredients. Depending on your preference, they vary in cost, and can often be purchased in bulk or in a package with mixed varieties. In combination with dried fruits and shredded, unsweetened coconut, mixed nuts can create a wonderful portable snack.

- **Herbs and Spices**. Consider your favorite foods and the spices they contain. This will give you a better idea of which options to include in your pantry, whether it's the hot spices of cayenne and chili, or a savorer variety, such as sage, curry, and cumin, or sweet options like cinnamon and cardamom. The more spices you collect, the easier it becomes to create new recipes and meals over time. When choosing a spice, you may choose to buy in bulk or in a jar. Once they are used up completely, keep the jars and label them, refilling will bulk or packaged spices. This will maximize the space you have and ensure you can keep an inventory of all the spices you have and anything you want to add. Dried herbs are stored in the same way, in small or medium-sized jars.

- **_Baking powder, baking soda, and Flours._** If you plan on baking, it's important to have the bare essential ingredients required in most recipes for bread, cakes, and pastries. Creating your own baked goods is a good alternative to store-bought options because you will save money and avoid unhealthy ingredients. Baking powder and baking soda are most often located in the baking section aisle of most grocery stores. The type of flour you choose depends on your allergies and any preferences you may have for your diet. For example, whole wheat flour is favored by many people, though due to gluten allergies and sensitivities, it can be replaced with other varieties of flour, such as potato flour, tapioca, almond and/or coconut flour. If you wish to reduce the level of carbohydrates in your diet, choosing coconut and almond flours are the best options, as they are low in carbs and high in nutrients.

1.3 Getting More Done With Less Effort

Designing a Plan for Where to Shop and How to Keep Your Kitchen Healthy for Easy Cooking and Food Prep

If you're going to shop for healthy, sustainable foods, and meal options, it will take some research and exploring to find the best places to shop for ingredients, groceries, and kitchen supplies. If you're already comfortable and familiar with your immediate area and the local shops, you may know where to find the most important items. Kitchen equipment, appliances, and utensils are often available at home improvement or department stores. Smaller specialty stores may also offer options, or if you are comfortable with online shopping, you'll have the benefit of comparing prices between different suppliers and stores.

The large grocery store chains are often most visible and offer most, if not all, items you'll need on your shopping list. Many grocers offer organic and local produce as an option in their stores, which makes it convenient and time-effective if you can't locate a local farmer's market nearby. Fortunately, most towns and cities have local markets that are typically open on Saturdays, and sometimes during the week during limited hours. If you have an opportunity, it's worthwhile to visit and shop at local markets, or making the effort to travel out of town to visit orchards, country markets and other sources of local foods. This will not only expand your shopping options, but it will also give you fresher, high-quality foods for your meal planning.

Keeping a clean and health-conscious kitchen is the key to avoiding bad habits and changing the way you approach food. Some of the most common problems in food preparation can be avoided with proper maintenance and cleanliness to avoid contamination. Prevention is the best option for all kitchen activities, especially the preparation of food:

- When you use a cutting board, always disinfect and wash it thoroughly after each use. Avoid mixing meat and vegetables or more than one item at a time (unless it is a mix of vegetables, such as garlic, onions, and peppers, for example). Meat is susceptible to contamination, especially when raw, and must be handled with the utmost care possible. Use separate cutting boards for meat and vegetables, just to avoid the spreading of bacteria, and clean the utensils, boards, and other items used immediately after.

- Store your meat in the refrigerator or freezer always. When you are ready to defrost the meat, move it to the refrigerator first one day in advance, before preparing for use. Some people leave a turkey or chicken on their countertop overnight to defrost, and while this may seem like a practical option, this method can invite the cultivation of unwanted bacteria and contamination. It may take longer to defrost in the refrigerator, though it is worth the extra effort and preventing any problems that may arise.

- Always wash your vegetables and fruits. Some pre-made salads or packages of carrots may claim to be "pre-washed," though this is no guarantee they are ready to eat out of the package. Salads are best made at home with fresh ingredients, so that you are aware of what's in them, and can avoid hidden sugars and additives, especially found in store-bought dressings. Apples and fruits with a thin layer of skin (unlike citrus fruits) should be thoroughly scrubbed. Some stores offer a special fruit and vegetable scrub that helps remove pesticides and other items on the coating of the skin.

- Don't leave cooked foods in a cooking pot overnight, even if they are covered. Some people may find it advantageous to leave a freshly stewed chili or gumbo soup in the cooking pot, covered overnight. This can be done for a short period of time, though not for more than an hour. As the food cools, it can become unhealthy to eat, and susceptible to spoilage or contamination. To prevent this from happening, store the food from the stovetop and store it in the refrigerator, in resealable containers. If you are creating a large batch of food that can provide enough for multiple people and several meals, create freezer portions as well, which can be reheated in the future.

- Keep your pantry items dry and cool. Never store dried foods in a moist area that has the likelihood of mold or other issues due to wetness. This includes cupboards and areas of the kitchen that may seem dry, though they should be avoided if they are in the direction of steam or cooking (above the stove) or near water sources (in, around or below the sink). Chances are, there will not be a leak or problem in most cases, though in the event there is a pipe burst or faucet leak, dried food stored under a sink can be ruined and unavailable for use.

- Store baked goods in a dry place, in the same way, grains and other pantry items, are stored. To keep bread, buns, and other baked goods fresher longer, store them in the refrigerator. Gluten-free bread is best kept in the freezer until ready for use. Whole-grain bread and baked goods containing sprouted grains and other natural ingredients should always be handled with care and refrigerated if you plan on keeping them for more than one day. If these foods are used within a day of buying them, they can be kept at room temperature, provided they are adequately covered and sealed to maintain freshness.

- Certain fruits can be stored at room temperatures, such as bananas, avocados, and some citrus fruits, though this is only good for a limited time, as they are perishable and will need to be used quickly. Bananas should be used as they ripen and can be consumed even when they are overripe. At this stage, they can be added to smoothies or baked into banana bread. Avocadoes tend to ripen quickly, and if not used soon after, can become overripe. Fortunately, they are acceptable slightly overripe and make a great dip or ingredient in salsa or guacamole.

- Clear and clean all kitchen surfaces when you are done the cooking, food preparation, or any other related work. This includes all surfaces: countertops, stovetop, and any additional surfaces in your kitchen. Disinfect thoroughly with a spray and scrub any signs of foods leftover, even trace amounts. Rinse and clean the sinks, and ensure no food or debris is flushed down the drain. Remove any peelings or other food scraps and deposit them into a compost or organics bin (if available). In your refrigerator, make a habit of wiping down all the shelves and compartments. Sometimes, foods leak or leave a residue, even long after they are consumed. This can result in cross-contamination or a negative impact on the freshness of other foods.

The greatest success you will have in your kitchen and with your diet is in maintaining your cooking and preparation spaces. When in doubt of the area, disinfect and clean, and always ensure the utensils, appliances, and equipment used are in good condition for the best quality possible. Hygiene is of the utmost importance in the kitchen and should be a priority at all times.

1.4 Cook on the weekend and Get Ready for the Week

Planning is a major advantage for sticking to a healthy diet, because it gives you more time to concentrate on your weekly work and family life, and less time to worry about what to eat. When you find yourself in a situation where you do not have the time or effort to cook or decide what to eat, reaching into the freezer or refrigerator for a ready-cooked meal can be the best solution. Creating a situation where you have home-cooked meals within reach and ready at any time is easier than you may think, though it does require some preparation and at least one day a week with an open schedule.

To begin planning for advance meal preparation, choose one day of the week, that is the most available and open for cooking. Select a day that gives you a minimum of six hours for preparation, if not more. This can be split up during the day, for example, three or four hours in the morning, and another three or four in the afternoon or evening. Make sure you budget your time and have all the equipment, appliances, and ingredients ready before you begin.

If you live alone, you can prepare one week of meals in advance easily, based on your own preferences and budget. If you have a household or family consisting of different preferences and meal ideas, this can be challenging, especially if not everyone is "on board" with healthy eating and meal preparation. In this case, planning a half or full-day "meal prep" is a good way to introduce new ideas, foods, and concepts to others, and allows them to join in and participate as well. In fact, weekly meal preparation can become a fun, enjoyable event, especially when collaborating and "cooking" up new ideas to include in your weekly meal plan.

If you decide to plan a weekly, healthy, meal preparation plan with family, roommates or neighbors, make sure you discuss some of the following items in advance, to avoid conflict and negative reactions:

- **Discuss food allergies and sensitivities.** If these are generally mild in nature and don't require the complete absence of certain foods, it's good to proceed with caution, to avoid unnecessary reactions and effects from certain foods. If someone in your family or group has a severe allergy, to nuts or seafood, for example, avoid these items completely and rinse all utensils and equipment prior to use if these foods have been included in recipes previously.

- **Are there any vegans or vegetarians in your family or group?** Some people who are vegetarian are comfortable with some dairy and/or egg products, and may not object to using utensils, cooking pots or skillets that may contain traces of meat. On the other hand, vegans are strictly animal-product free and preparing vegan meals or options would require a separate set of utensils and ingredients. This should be discussed in detail beforehand, to ensure everyone involved is agreeable to how the meal planning will work. For example, a compromise may be reached that provides "meat-free" meals and others with the option of dairy and/or meat. Customizing your weekly meals can take some time and creativity, though it's a great way to explore different options and try new ways of cooking.

- **Some people are eager to try any type of food or dish available, while others are hesitant and not keen on new meal options.** Creating a meal plan should be an opportunity to explore new tastes and ideas, though if anyone is resistant, it can be a challenge. If this is the case, try approaching them with the types of foods they already enjoy, and suggest new changes or ingredient options. For example, a lasagna or casserole dish can be altered in many ways to create new flavors and meals every time. This type of meal is a good option for picky eaters to try something new that resembles a familiar food they may enjoy.

- **_Encourage a sense of adventure when it comes to food._** Some people are afraid to try something new because it may look unusual or seem, unlike anything they have tried before. For example, some people may avoid sushi because of the mere mention of raw fish, without realizing it's much more than that. Sometimes a specific fruit or vegetable doesn't appeal to someone because they haven't tried it in a delicious recipe and have no clue how it really tastes. Not all foods taste the way they are perceived to, and at the very least, trying a new food once is a good way to expand your palate and invite new flavors and textures into your regular meals.

For most people, the weekend offers a good time frame to fit a few hours of meal preparation, which is good for a typical work week. The meal prep should consist of dinners mostly so that they can be easily warmed and enjoyed throughout the week. Breakfast can be easily prepared in the morning, such as eggs and hot cereal, or the night before, such as overnight oatmeal. Some breakfast and lunch meals can be prepared one week in advance or as a part of the previous day's dinner, which can be brought to school or work as lunch. Meal preparation offers many options that can be customized to fit within your schedule, and it works, as long as it becomes and remains a consistent part of your week.

Chapter 2: Heal the Immune System

2.1 Top 20 Healthy Foods

The Best Foods for Your Diet

To get the most out of your diet, be selective, and find the foods you love to eat, which are also good for you. Often, healthy foods are considered bland or lacking the taste and texture we might be accustomed to with deep-fried and sweet, sugary foods. This is because we haven't adapted to the wide range of taste experience of natural, whole foods that we can learn to enjoy. For example, if we consume too much soda, we may not appreciate the natural sweetness of a mango or the tart, yet sweet combination in berries and the tangy taste if citrus fruits. Many of the processed food we include in our diet is based and created from natural foods. It's important to focus on the root sources, such as fresh tomatoes instead of ketchup, or a ripe avocado instead of premade guacamole.

There is a group of foods known as "superfoods" for their high levels of nutrients, and the numerous benefits these have on our health. All-natural foods contain nutrients that we require as part of our daily needs, though "superfoods" offer you a lot more in a smaller amount. Combining just a few of these in one meal can satisfy your daily requirements. Some of these foods may be familiar, while others are less common. Fortunately, as there are more studies conducted and benefits learned about these powerful foods, they will grow in popularity, becoming more frequently available in standard grocery stores.

- *Avocados.* Most popular as an ingredient in guacamole, or in sushi rolls, avocado is rich in omega 3 and 6s, fiber, and low in carbohydrates. This fruit provides the nutritional value of healthy fats and vitamins, with a dose of fiber. It's a staple in ketogenic and low carb diets, which focus on increasing the number of healthy fats while reducing carbohydrates. Avocadoes are a great addition to other diets as well, such as plant-based and paleo diets, which focus on whole foods with minimal or no processing

- *Chia seeds.* The spotlight has recently been on these tiny seeds for their limitless potential in boosting health with the high amount of nutrients they contain. Chia seeds are versatile and neutral in taste, which makes them an ideal addition to many dishes and recipes. When they are soaked overnight in milk or yogurt, they become softened and jelly-like. In cereals and granola recipes, they mix well and complement the flavors included in the mix. They are considered superfoods due to the high volume of nutrients, which include calcium, protein, antioxidants, and fiber. Just one small portion can provide a significant boost to your diet.

- *Kale.* Of all the dark, leafy green vegetables, kale is the most nutrient-dense of them. Bitter to taste, and often overlooked because of its rough texture and flavor, kale can be easily added to many dishes or prepared as a side dish. Once it is baked, cooked, or steamed, this vegetable's flavor tends to mellow and blend in with other foods cooked with it, such as garlic, onions, sea salt, and oil. Kale contains high levels of calcium, iron, protein, and fiber. It's also rich in antioxidants.

- **Coconut Oil.** A source of natural fat, coconut oil is a highly beneficial oil to include in your recipes and can be added to smoothies and desserts. MCT oil is a purer form of the fat content contained with coconut oil and often used to supplement drinks and meals to increase the number of healthy fats in a diet.

- **Fish.** Salmon and other varieties of fatty fish are the best options, as they are very high in healthy oils and fats, and low in carbohydrates. Seafood contains a significant source of protein and compliments a side of salad or roasted vegetables. Fish can be enjoyed in its raw form, like sushi or sashimi, or baked or steamed on a bed of brown rice or salad.

- **Berries.** Strawberries, raspberries, blueberries, cherries, and blackberries are full of antioxidants, including vitamin C, which helps prevent cancer. Antioxidants also block or stop the growth of free radicals, which cause cancerous growth.

- ***Olive oil.*** Commonly used to fry or sauté, olive oil is a good source of healthy fats, and a valuable ingredient in homemade salad dressings, dips, and marinades. It's best consumed in its raw form to reap the best of the health benefits.

- ***Almonds.*** All nuts are healthy and are recommended for a well-balanced diet, and while each variety contains high amounts of fiber and protein, almonds are the most nutrient-rich, containing multiple daily requirements of protein and fiber in just one small handful. As a topping on salads, crushed into a smoothie, or as a snack, almonds are delicious and easy to enjoy because of their tasty flavor. They are best enjoyed raw or lightly toasted and make an excellent option for snacking on the go.

- ***Asparagus.*** This spear-shaped, green vegetable is flavorful and full of fiber and vitamins. It's excellent for any meal of the day and can be boiled, baked, or fried.

- ***Tofu and Tempeh.*** Soy food products are the main staple in most vegan and plant-based diets. Vitamin B12, a nutrient usually found only in red meat, is in miso (fermented soybean paste, used to make soup) and tempeh, another fermented soy. Tofu is versatile and can be used in everything from soup, skillet dishes, bakes, and desserts. All soy contains a high amount of protein, fiber, and calcium.

- **Mushrooms.** Portobello, button mushrooms, shitake, and many more varieties are full of more nutrients than you may expect. Fiber, potassium, protein, and other vitamins are located in a variety of different mushrooms. They are easily added to a wide variety of dishes, including using portobello mushrooms for burgers, to slicing and mixing with vegetables for stir fry dishes.

- **Sprouts.** Include as many sprouts as possible, as they are strong and full of vitamins in their raw form and can make a great addition to wraps and salads. Mustard seeds, bean sprouts, and other types of sprouts can be found in some local grocery stores and farmers' markets. They are loaded with enzymes, fiber, and chlorophyll. Some stores sell kits with seeds and materials to grow your own sprouts. This has become popular in recent years due to the number of positive health benefits of these foods.

- **Broccoli.** One of the top foods that fight against cancer, and a tasty option for many bakes and casseroles, broccoli contains a significant source of fiber, iron, vitamin K, C, and potassium.

- **Tomatoes.** Like broccoli, tomatoes are among a group of foods that are known for their anti-cancer properties and work well in a number of dishes, either raw, stewed, or baked. All varieties of tomatoes are high in nutrients and contain a significant number of antioxidants.

- **Squash.** There are many different types of squash, and all of them are worth adding to your diet because of their taste, various uses, and vitamins. Squash contains a strong amount of beta carotene (vitamin A), which is good for eye and vision health. Squash also contains fiber, magnesium, phosphorus, vitamin B6, and many other nutrients.

- **Cashew Nuts.** These are high in protein and work in many recipes as a topping or added ingredient. They are high in protein, fiber, and omega 3 and 6s, and tasty as a treat on their own, while ideal in a trail mix.

- **Bananas.** A perfect meal on their own, bananas provides just the right energy with potassium, fiber, and a bit of protein to start your day. They make an excellent ingredient for smoothies and combine well with many other fruits and milk options.

- **Apples.** An ideal source of fiber and vitamin C, apples are a great snack on their own, in a sauce, butter, or baked dessert. There are many types of apples, and while they all have different flavors, their nutrient level is similar and beneficial all the same.

- **Hemp Seeds.** Over recent years, hemp seeds, most commonly available as hemp "hearts" are known for their strong levels of omega 3 and 6s, and protein. They can be crushed into powder form and used as a supplement in smoothies and energy bars.

- ***Flax Seeds.*** Like hemp seeds, flax is another nutrient-rich seed that gives your body a lot of nutrients, even in a small dose. Crushed or powdered flax seeds combined with water is often used as a replacement for eggs in many vegan recipes.

2.2 Top 20 Junk Foods

Top Foods to Avoid

Improving your health and eating habits involves eliminating the foods in your current diet that are processed, high in artificial ingredients and refined sugars. Some junk food may appear beneficial, due to a certain brand or product claims, though often there are hidden items that cause more harm, with little or no nutritional value. Often, we may come across processed foods in the grocery store that is packaged and labeled as healthy and natural, which is far from accurate. While consuming these foods on occasion isn't going to have a major impact on your health, it's easy to develop a habit for eating them regularly, and best to avoid completely.

- **Sports drinks, sodas, and fruit juices.** Soda, sports drinks, and fruit juices are loaded in refined sugars, and often with the addition of artificial flavors. Just one drink contains more than ten teaspoons of added sugar, and a can of soda can reach close to twenty teaspoons. Often, drinking sugary beverages is habit-forming and it's not easy to quit overnight. Diet sodas contain artificial sweeteners to replace the sugar, which have negative side effects of their own and should be avoided. With the exception of a few select naturally sweetened or low carb sweetened sparkling beverages, soda, and sugary drinks should be avoided. Choose sparkling water, natural iced tea, homemade squeezed juices (vegetable and/or fruit), natural coffee, and water.

- **Deep-fried foods (hamburgers, French fries).** Fast food outlets are famous for their hamburgers and French fries. While variations to hamburgers may seem healthier in some restaurants, due to the quality of the meat and clean kitchen practices, or meat-free options and naturally raised beef, the overall effect of eating fried or deep-fried foods are negative. The impact on your health includes an increase in heart disease, clogged arteries, and high blood pressure. The best alternative to deep-fried foods is boiled, steamed, or baked. Consider a baked potato or yam in place of French fries or lean roast beef instead of a burger.

- *Chips and crackers.* Potato chips and crackers are often served or enjoyed as snacks, though most people don't realize the high levels of sodium, artificial flavors, and other ingredients they contain. These ingredients not only contribute to higher risks associated with blood pressure and sugar levels; they also increase weight gain that leads to obesity. Many packaged varieties of these snacks claim "all-natural ingredients," "low sodium" or "no added sugar," though in general, they provide little or no nutritional value, and are used as a filler or supplement to other ingredients, such as cheese, vegetable, and meat-based spreads. In place of crackers or chips, consider enjoying raw vegetables and dip, such as hummus, eggplant dip, or other low carb or healthy cheese dips.

- **Sweetened Yogurt and Cream Cheese.** Dairy products, in their natural, unsweetened state, are beneficial in moderation. However, most dairy products contain sugar, hidden artificial ingredients, and fruit flavoring that's unnatural. Lactose is a natural sugar found in milk and dairy products, though often fructose (fruit sugar) and refined sweeteners are added. If you enjoy dairy as part of your diet, choose low fat and unsweetened versions of yogurt, cheese, and milk. Natural sweeteners and fruit can be added to plain versions of yogurt and cream cheese for added flavor, without the need for additives or artificial ingredients. Goat cheese and other spreadable cheese options are often sweetened or flavored with high sodium levels. It's best to steer clear of all flavored dairy products.

- **Smoked Meats.** Often enjoyed for their strong and distinct flavor, smoked meats are high in sodium, nitrates, and carcinogens. Regular consumption of these meats creates an increased risk of heart ailments, disease, cancer, and weight gain. Many people add these meats to their sandwiches for lunch, or buy them at fast-food restaurants, without much consideration for their impact on health. Most sliced meats in the deli section of a grocery store are culprits of hidden high levels of sodium and preservatives that serve no value to a healthy diet. Choose instead lean, frozen meats that are already baked or ready to bake or cook without deep frying. Some cheese and vegan meat alternatives are smoked and carry the same or similar risk to your health.

- **White rice, bread, and other refined foods.** Refined foods are low in nutrients, providing little to no value in your diet. They are often considered "filler" foods, in that they are consumed to conquer hunger without sustenance, and as a result, could delay the sensation of fullness, which results in overeating. Another reason many people buy these foods is that they are often inexpensive and easy to add to meals. Realistically, the long-term eating habits that include a significant volume of refined foods will result in nutrient deficiencies and excessive weight gain. They are also high in carbohydrates and hidden sugars, which spikes the level of blood sugar, while there is a higher risk of type 2 diabetes, which can develop.

- **_Ice Cream._** Store-bought ice cream options are often full of sugar, artificial color, and additives that cause long-term harm to your health. While there are some healthier versions of frozen treats, whether they are non-dairy, low carb, or low sugar, most ice cream varieties should be avoided for their ingredients. Fortunately, creating your own ice cream is an easy process and a worthwhile project to try in the warmer season. You'll have the option of using all-natural ingredients and creating any flavor or combination of tastes you enjoy.

- **_Boxed Cereals._** Once considered a healthy option for breakfast, it was soon discovered that many prepared, cold bowls of cereal were full of high fructose corn syrup, an ingredient that raised the sugar levels in your body to an extreme level, and also responsible for excessive weight gain and other health issues due to regular consumption. Many of the ingredients listed in these products are limited, and not substantial to benefit a healthy way of eating. While they are convenient and easy to use often, they can also be expensive and addictive, due to their high sugar levels. As an alternative, replace with homemade granola or substitute with a bowl of yogurt, fruit, and various nuts and seeds for a healthy breakfast.

- **Frozen Entrees.** This is added to the list due to the number of frozen dinners that contain a high amount of preservatives. However, some products are less problematic and maybe enjoyed on occasion. In most cases, frozen fried foods, French fries, and ready-made meals should be avoided as much as possible. Instead, buy frozen whole foods, such as lean meats, vegetables, and dairy products. If the frozen meal you decide to purchase was created by a local farmer or chef, then it may be an exception to the general rule and enjoyed as part of your diet.

- **Canned Fruits and Syrups.** These foods can be tempting as a topping or a treat, though should be avoided. The syrups contained in canned fruits contain excessive amounts of sugar and provide no benefits for your diet. The fruits contained in these canned have lost most of their nutrients due to the preservatives.

- **Chemically Dried Fruit**. Not all dried fruit is prepared the same, and while it should be sun-dried for best results, many types found in stores and markets are chemically dried, which alters the quality of the fruit. Always be cautious and stick with naturally sun-dried fruit for best results and no additives.

- **Canned foods**. These should be avoided as much as possible, due to the levels of preservatives and chemicals added to them. Vegetables, fruits, and other foods canned are often far less nutritious than their frozen or fresh counterparts. Canned foods have less flavor and should only be used in situations where fresh and frozen options are not available.

- **Bacon**. It's a tasty option for many breakfast meals, though bacon is high in trans-fat when fried, and doesn't contain any nutrients that are beneficial for your health.

- ***Flavored sauces.*** Many sauces and dips can be tempting in the spice aisle, especially when you're preparing a barbeque or creating a baked dish or stew. Always keep in mind that most, if not all, sauces contain artificial flavors and sugars, which are counterproductive to healthy eating. Fortunately, you can create most of these on your own with simple recipes that contain all-natural ingredients.

- ***Store-bought Salad Dressings***. Like sauces and dips available in-store, salad dressings are also culprits for high sugar and artificial flavors, even where they boast all-natural ingredients. Balsamic and vinegar-based dressings are ideal and recommended for salads and can be easily made from scratch.

- ***Chocolate Milk and Non-Dairy Milk.*** On some occasions, chocolate or flavored milk, whether it's dairy or non-dairy, can contain natural ingredients, though, for the most part, they are high in sugar and carbs. For best results, choose all-natural milk and add your own dark cocoa powder or melted dark chocolate. Avoid using processed foods, including milk, as much as possible, to skip the hidden sugar and syrups they contain.

- **Salted Nuts and Seeds.** While eating nuts and seeds is ideal and encouraged for a healthy diet, many varieties are high in sodium, which is unhealthy. Avoid this completely by choosing raw or lightly roasted nuts and seeds, and skip the salt completely, or add just a dash of your own sea salt.

- **Dessert Whipped Topping.** High fructose corn syrup is an ingredient that should be avoided at all costs, due to its negative impact on health, and its high level of sugar. It's been shown to increase weight gain, cause health problems, and contribute to obesity. It's usually found in boxed cereals and other dessert toppings and options, including whipped toppings, which are not always dairy or vegetable-based, but completely unnatural and full of additives. Instead of this option, use all-natural whipping cream.

- **Pastries and baked goods.** Unless you are making your own baked goods, avoid any store-

bought pastries, pies, or cakes, as they are
loaded with artificial ingredients and high in
sugar. Instead, find a local bakery with all-
natural options (including gluten-free, vegan,
and/or ketogenic options) or try making your own
version of your favorite baked goods.

- **Fruit Juices.** Like soda, fruit juice is full of sugar
and without much benefit to your health. Any of
the claims of vitamins and fiber get lost in the
additives, food coloring, and artificial flavors often
contained in a variety of juices. On the other
hand, squeezing or pressing your own juices is
rewarding a much healthier.

2.3 Including Fruits and Vegetables in Your Diet

The best way to ensure you're getting the most out of a
healthy diet is to increase the number of fruits and
vegetables you consume on a regular basis. This
means ensuring you meet your daily nutrient
requirements, and beyond. Most

The Nutrients and Benefits of Fruits and Vegetables

All vegetables and fruits contain a wealth of nutrients and are vital for maintaining your daily requirements. Expanding the variety and choices if foods you include in your diet is one of the nest methods for maintaining good health and preventing disease. When you visit the local farmer's market, you'll notice a wide variety of choice, most (if not all) are locally grown and freshly harvested.

The best advantage of fresh vegetables and fruits? They are all-natural and full of nutrients, regardless of your preference for taste and texture. Always feel free to choose widely from these foods, as they are all great options, and can be applied or used in a variety of snacks and recipes.

Chapter 3: First Week Healthy Meal Prep

3.1 Shopping List and Explanations

Creating a shopping list requires organizing your ingredients, food choices, and alternatives well in advance, to make your experience worthwhile and well-thought-out. Organizing your shopping list over the weekend is especially helpful for shopping and meal preparation, which is also done on Saturday and/or Sunday, in preparation for the following week. Creating this list is more than the items you plan to buy; it serves as a template for your staple items, with the option of adding or substituting some items with alternatives if some of the foods chosen are unavailable. For example, you may include peaches as an option on your list, and notice they are no longer available or sold out. At that point, you may decide to buy apples or mangoes instead. If the peaches are for a snack only, this decision can be made on the spot. However, if they are part of a recipe, it may be beneficial to find an alternative fruit or ingredient that can best replace it.

3.1.1 Monday

This chapter covers the first of the three-week meal healthy meal prep plan. During the initial week, there is a focus on plant-based foods, with some dairy and egg options, while shifting more towards vegan and vegetarian meals. This allows the body to cleanse, recharge, and start with a new variety of food options that expand your palate. Some of the foods will be familiar, such as berries, eggs, and toast, while others may or may not be as common in your current diets, such as chia seeds, avocado, and soy products. The benefit of the first week is exploring these new tastes while getting used to a healthier way of eating. You may notice some results after this week is done, such as:

- Higher levels of energy

- Faster metabolism and regularity

- Craving for new and different flavors not previously experienced before

During the first week of the meal prep planning, you'll need to include the following items in your shopping list, as they are included in all of the recipes:

- 1 package of chia seeds (any variety, color)

- 2 cans of coconut milk

- 1 small or medium container of vanilla extract (there are both natural and artificial options – choose the natural option)

- 1 jar of honey or container of maple syrup

- 1 small or medium carton of cream or coconut cream (dairy or non-dairy)

- 1 bag of mixed frozen or carton of fresh berries

- 2 large mangoes

- 2 lemon or limes

- 1 large chicken (add to the freezer)

- 2-3 varieties of beans (kidney beans, chickpeas, black beans, fava beans and/or pinto beans)

- 1 jar of tahini butter

- 1 jar of peanut butter

- 1 package, or the equivalent of 3 cups of chia seeds

- 1 can of coconut cream or carton of dairy cream

- 1 large bottle of olive oil

- Cilantro, parsley, dill, and other fresh herbs and green vegetables

- Squash (2-3 varieties, including pumpkin)

Other considerations for your shopping list: add an assortment of spices and seasonings to your pantry, including cumin, sea salt, black pepper, chili pepper, cayenne, dill, paprika, oregano, and other spices. Check the recipes over the three week period to determine which options you need and prefer, where there are choices available.

Breakfast: Chia Seed Pudding with Berries

Chia seeds contain high amounts of protein, calcium, and fiber. This pudding creates a naturally sweet and nutrient-rich breakfast that can be easily prepared the night before and enjoyed the next morning. Berries are added to boost the antioxidant levels in this delicious meal. Chia seeds are easy to store, and only a small amount is required for 2 servings.

- 1 ¼ cups of coconut milk

- ¼ cup of natural dairy or coconut cream

- ½ cups of chia seeds (any variety)

- 2 teaspoons of maple syrup or honey

- ½ tablespoons of vanilla extract

- ½ cup of fresh or frozen berries (any variety or a mix of berries)

Combine the coconut milk, cream, vanilla extract, and sweetener in a medium-sized bowl. Whisk thoroughly until well mixed. Fold in the chia seeds and blend until the seeds are evenly spaced. Gently fold in the berries and pour the pudding mix into a sealable container. Refrigerate overnight and service in the morning.

Toppings for this recipe include additional fresh berries, crushed peanuts or sliced almonds and sliced banana. A light dusting of cocoa powder or cinnamon can also be added.

Lunch: Roast Turkey Wrap with Greens and Mustard

If you're looking for an easy meal to create for lunch, this is an ideal and tasty wrap. When choosing turkey meat, make sure it is oven roasted, without any further processing or additives. Leftover turkey breast from a roast dinner can also be included as an option.

- 2 slices of sliced turkey (baked) or leftover roasted meat

- 1 teaspoon of mustard

- ½ cup of sprouts (alfalfa and/or mustard seed)

- 3 sprigs of arugula

- Dash of black pepper

- 1 large wrap

- 1 sliced bell pepper

- ½ cup of diced cucumber

Place the wrap on a plate, and lightly coat is mustard. Add turkey meat, sprouts, arugula, bell pepper, and cucumber, then sprinkle with black pepper and roll up the wrap. Grill for less than one minute, then serve

Snacks: Mango Salad

An easy and delicious snack to create, mango salad contains a medley of flavors that satisfies hunger and a craving for good taste. This dish is prepared without any cooking or baking, which makes it ideal for quick preparation and enjoyment. This dish is an excellent side option or a light lunch.

- 1 cup of cashews (raw, unsalted)

- 2 small or medium mangoes (not too ripe; firm enough to slice)

- ¼ cup of fresh mint

- ½ cup of shredded lettuce

- 1 tablespoon of balsamic vinegar

- ½ cup of shredded carrots

- 2 tablespoons of lemon juice

- Fresh cilantro, sliced

- 3 teaspoons of olive oil

- ½ bell pepper, thinly sliced, lengthwise

- ½ of red onion sliced thinly

- 1 small or medium tomato, diced

- 1 teaspoon of maple syrup or honey

- ½ teaspoon of sea salt

- Dash of black pepper

Mix the mangoes, mint, lettuce, carrots, onions, tomato, and pepper in a bowl. Combine thoroughly to ensure all ingredients are well combined. Prepare the dressing: mix the balsamic vinegar, lemon juice, and olive oil in a separate bowl, then add the salt and pepper. Stir in the maple syrup or honey. Pour and mix over the salad, add fresh cilantro, and serve.

Dinner: Curried Cabbage and Potato Soup

This is a healthy and hearty soup that only requires a handful of ingredients to enjoy. The cabbage is lightly sautéed on the stovetop and flavored with curry, in preparation for the soup, which is created with a vegetable broth base, potatoes, and spices. This soup is easy to prepare and freeze or refrigerate in portions for several meals:

- 3 large or 4 medium-sized potatoes

- 3 ½ or 4 cups of vegetable broth

- 2 teaspoons of curry powder

- 1 teaspoon of crushed or dried ginger root

- Dash of sea salt

- ½ tablespoon of black pepper

- 1 cup of shredded cabbage

- ½ tablespoon of garam masala

- 2 tablespoons of olive oil

- ½ tablespoon of garlic

- 2 teaspoons of crushed onions

Heat the olive oil in a skillet on medium level heat, then add the onions and cabbage. Sautee for 5-6 minutes, then add in the curry powder, garam masala, garlic, onions, black pepper, and sea salt. Simmer for a few minutes longer, until all vegetables are tender. Remove the skillet from the stovetop to cool. Bring the vegetable broth to a boil in a cooking pot and add in the black pepper and sea salt. Scrub and wash the potatoes, removing the skin and slicing into small, one-inch pieces. Add to the cooking pot to boil. Cook on high heat to boil and continue to cook for ten minutes, then cook covered medium heat for 20-30 minutes, or as long as it takes for the potatoes to soften. Remove from the stovetop, and cool slightly, then blend the vegetable broth and potato mix in batches. This will result in a thick, potato-based soup. Return to the cooking pot and stir in the curried cabbage. Heat and stir the ingredients together, test-tasting, and adding more spices and sea salt as needed. This recipe makes approximately four servings.

When freezing this soup for later use, allow it to cool completely, then divide into equal portions, or freeze together in one container.

3.1.2 Tuesday

Breakfast: Tofu and Spinach Breakfast Bowl

Tofu is the main feature in a vegan or plant-based diet. It's a versatile form of soy that can be used in many types of meals and recipes. Like eggs, tofu can be scrambled and spiced or seasoned in a variety of ways. This dish includes a few spice options.

- 1 block of extra firm tofu

- 2 teaspoons of turmeric

- 1 small onion, diced

- 2 cups of broth (vegetable, beef or chicken)

- ½ tablespoon of pepper

- ½ teaspoon of cumin

- Dash of sea salt

- ½ teaspoon of chili powder

- ½ teaspoon of curry powder

- 2-3 bay leaves

- 1 cup of cooked or frozen spinach

- 5-6 cherry tomatoes, sliced in half

- ½ cup of cucumber, diced

- 2 tablespoons of lemon juice

- 3 teaspoons of olive oil

- Fresh dill

To prepare the tofu for this meal, it's best to marinate overnight, by combining the broth, black pepper, turmeric, chili pepper, cumin, bay leaves and curry powder in a resealable container. Drain and rinse the tofu, then slice into cubes and place in the broth. Marinate for a minimum of two hours. For best results, soak overnight and use it in the morning. Once the tofu is ready to use, drain from the broth, retaining ¼ cup, and heat a skillet with olive oil on medium heat. Mash the tofu in a separate bowl. Add in ½ teaspoon of turmeric, together with sea salt and black pepper. Add the tofu and onions to the skillet and cook like scrambled eggs for 2-3 minutes, then add spinach. Defrost the spinach if frozen, for one minute in the microwave, and add to the tofu. Scramble together bd serve in a bowl topped with cherry tomatoes, sliced cucumbers, and dill. To create the dressing, mix the lemon juice and olive oil, whisking together in a bowl, then drizzle over the bowl. Add fresh cilantro or parsley, as an option.

Lunch: Curried Squash Soup

If you have always wanted to try squash in a recipe, this is the ideal opportunity to give it a shot. Butternut and acorn squash are both common to use, though any type of squash can be used as desired. The curry is created with a coconut milk base and is mild in flavor, yet strong enough to boost the natural aroma of the squash.

- 1 medium-sized squash, any variety

- 3 teaspoons of curry powder

- 2 cups of coconut milk

- 3 ½ cups of broth (vegetable or chicken)

- 1 teaspoon of sea salt

- 1 clove of garlic, crushed

- 1 teaspoon of fresh or ground ginger

- 1 small onion, diced

- ½ tablespoon of black pepper

- 1 carrot, sliced

- Olive oil for cooking

Heat the olive oil in a medium-sized skillet, then add in the onion, garlic, ginger, and spices. Cook for 3-4 minutes, then add the chopped carrots. Simmer for 4 or 5 minutes on low-medium heat, then set aside to cool. In a preheated oven, bake the squash for 45 minutes, until the inside flesh is tender. Scoop out the flesh and separate the seeds, adding the squash to the skillet ingredients. Combine all ingredients from the skillet and transfer to a large cooking pot. Add the four cups of vegetable stock and cook until boiling on medium. Stir in the two cups of coconut milk, and additional curry spice as needed (another 2 teaspoons). Add the remaining spices and stew on low-medium for 13-15 minutes, then remove to cool.

Pour the soup into a food processor or blender and mix in batches and mix until everything is smooth and without any lumps. Return to the large cooking pot to reheat, then serve.

Snacks: Spicy Roasted Squash Seeds

If you are tempted to discard the squash seeds from the recipe above, reconsider using them for this recipe. Creating spicy, oven-roasted squash seeds is an ideal way to create a healthy snack and avoid food waste.

- 1 – 1 ½ cups of raw squash seeds

- 1 teaspoon of sea salt

- 1 teaspoon of chili pepper

- 2 teaspoons of olive oil

- Dash of black pepper

Prepare a baking tray and coat lightly with olive oil. In a small bowl, mix the spices together. Lightly coat all the seeds in olive oil. Spread the seeds on the baking sheet. Sprinkle the spice mix over the seeds. Preheat the oven to 300 degrees and cook for 15-20 minutes, until golden, but not burnt. Remove and cool before serving

Dinner: Shepherd's Pie with Yams

This recipe is a twist on the traditional Shepherd's pie, where the potatoes are switches for yams, and there is a spicier taste to the overall dish. For the vegan or vegetarian option, replace the ground beef with soy meat.

- 3-4 yams, washed and peeled

- 2 cups of ground beef (extra lean) or soy meat (as a vegan or vegetarian option)

- 1 teaspoon of chili

- 1 onion, diced

- ¾ cups of corn (fresh or frozen)

- ¾ cups of green peas (fresh or frozen)

- 1 celery stalk, diced

- ½ tablespoon of black pepper

- 1 bell pepper, chopped

- 1 carrot, diced into small pieces

- 2 cloves of crushed garlic

- 3 teaspoons of olive oil

- 2 teaspoons flour

- 1/8 cup of water

- ½ tablespoon of garlic powder

- ½ tablespoon of paprika

- 1 tablespoon of cream

- 1/8 cup of butter

Prepare a large skillet with olive oil to heat and add the extra lean ground beef. Cook for 15 minutes until the meat is well done, then add in the garlic, onion, bell pepper, chili pepper, sea salt, and black pepper. Simmer for ten more minutes, then reduce to medium-low and add in the carrots, celery, peas, and corn. Stir gently to fold the vegetables into the mix, then add in the flour and water, mixing thoroughly. Set aside to cool for ten minutes.

Prepare a casserole dish and heat the oven at 375 degrees. Scoop the meat and vegetable mix from the skillet and evenly spread in the dish. Prepare the yams by slicing into small, one-inch pieces, and add to a medium cooking pot with water. Boil the water, then add sea salt. Cook until softened, then remove, drain, add cream and butter, then mash. An electric mixer will create a smoother result. Coat the potatoes on top of the meat, then sprinkle lightly with garlic powder, black pepper, and paprika. Bake for 30-40 minutes, or until lightly golden on top. This meal serves 4-6.

3.1.3 Wednesday

Breakfast: Poached Eggs on Avocado

Eggs are a healthy source of fats, protein, and calcium, and work well as a breakfast food due to the significant nutrient boost, they provide. Poached eggs are prepared by dropping one egg at a time in boiling water and allowing it to cook fully, before scooping it out with a slotted spoon and serving. In this dish, two eggs are poached and served with firm, slightly ripened avocado, sliced on whole-grain toast.

- 2 eggs (large or medium)

- 1 large avocado (not too ripe, slightly firm)

- 2 slices of rye or whole-grain bread

- 1 teaspoon of natural butter

Boil two cups of water in a cooking pot, then add a dash of sea salt. Once the water is brought to a boil, crack one egg open at a time, and drop into the water, cooking for several minutes. The egg white may spread slightly in the water around the yolks. As the eggs cook, toast two slices of whole-grain toast and add a thin layer of butter. Pit and remove the peeling from one large avocado, and slice thinly, coating each slice in layers. Top with the poached eggs once they are done, and sprinkle with black pepper.

Lunch: Couscous, Parsley and Bean Salad

Couscous is a popular grain in many Middle Eastern and Mediterranean dishes. It's mild to take and combines well with other flavors and textures, to create a full meal. Kidney beans are added to this salad for their high protein and fiber, while parsley is added for vitamins and antioxidants. The dressing is tangy and works well with the combination of ingredients.

- 1 cup of kidney beans (pre-soaked and cooked)

- 2 cups of cooked couscous

- 1 teaspoon of sage

- 1 cup of finely diced parsley

- 2 teaspoons of lime juice

- 3 ½ teaspoons of olive oil

- 1 teaspoon of dried rosemary

- ½ tablespoon of dried or fresh dill

Cook the couscous following the directions, then set aside to cool. Mix in a medium bowl with kidney beans, parsley, sage, and dill. In a separate bowl, mix lime juice, olive oil, and rosemary. Drizzle the dressing over the salad, mix, and serve. For a sweet variation, add a handful of dried cranberries.

Snacks: Peanut Butter Squares

This is a raw, bake-free snack that can be prepared conveniently within a few minutes. The base of this recipe is high protein: peanut butter and oats. Almond flour and sweetener are also added for additional flavor.

- 1 cup of peanut butter, smooth, at room temperature

- 1 cup of raw oats

- 2 teaspoons low carb syrup or maple syrup

- ¾ cup of almond flour

Mix the oats and almond flour in a bowl. In a separate mixing bowl, mash the peanut butter with the sweetener. Combine both sets of ingredients together until the dough has a thick consistency. Prepare a baking dish and transfer the mixture into the pan, coating evenly. Refrigerate for two hours minimum, then slice and serve.

Dinner: Homemade Gnocchi

If you want to sample a hearty pasta treat, this is a fun and simple meal to create from scratch. Only three main ingredients are required: potatoes, wheat flour, and eggs. Gluten-Free flour can be substituted for flour.

- 2 cups of whole wheat flour

- 2 large potatoes

- 1 egg

Wash and peel the potatoes, then slice into cubes and add to 3 cups of water. Add a dash of salt to the water. Boil the water, then cook potatoes until they are tender. Drain and mash the potatoes and add in the flour and egg. Make sure the potatoes have cooled slightly after being mashed, to prevent the egg from "cooking" when it is mixed in with the other ingredients. Create a smooth dough and roll on a cutting board into log one-inch logs, and slice one or one and a half-inch bites. Fill a freshly cleaned cooking pot, pour half of the pot with water, add sea salt and boil. Gently drop the gnocchi in and continue to cook on high for another 4-5 minutes, then drain, and serve.

There are several ways to enjoy gnocchi, with one of the most popular with tomato sauce and cheese. To prepare the tomato sauce, pour two cups of pureed tomatoes into a small cooking pot and simmer on medium, stirring in oregano, paprika, chili pepper, black pepper, and salt. Add some thyme, sage and other spices as desired, such as crushed garlic and/or onion. Stew for 15 minutes, then pours over gnocchi and cover in shredded cheese or feta.

3.1.4 Thursday

Breakfast: Overnight Oatmeal

This is a meal best prepared the night before and can last up to 2-3 days in the refrigerator for best results. Regular oats are used, in combination with your choice of dairy or non-dairy milk and toppings. This recipe allows for several options, beginning with a basic three-ingredient recipe:

- ½ cup of steel-cut oats

- 1 cup of milk (low fat or non-dairy milk, such as soy, almond or coconut)

- 3 teaspoons of maple syrup or honey

In a small or medium-sized jar, pour in the raw oats so that they sit at the bottom of the jar, then pour the milk over top and top with the maple syrup or honey. Refrigerate overnight, then remove in the morning, stir and enjoy. Other options for preparing overnight oatmeal include the following:

- Add two teaspoons of peanut butter or hazelnut butter, one teaspoon of cocoa powder as a topping. In the morning, add one sliced banana and serve

- Top with shredded coconut and use coconut milk. In the morning, add ½ cup of fresh or dried pineapple slices, additional shredded or sliced coconut and berries

- Replace or add yogurt to the milk and mix in one cup of assorted berries to the jar when preparing for the refrigerator overnight.

Lunch: Egg and Tofu Fried Rice

When most people think of tofu, they might consider it as strictly for vegans, without giving it much thought as part of their meal plan. While tofu is a staple in a plant-based diet, it's also an excellent ingredient in many dishes, some including meat such as ma po tofu, a popular Asian dish that combines pork and tofu. Pad Thai is another dish that combines tofu, egg, chicken, and shrimp. There are many options and meal variations that include soy, whether there is meat, egg, or neither. In this dish, tofu is pan-seared in sesame oil, then cooked with the rice.

- 2 cups of cooked (steamed) rice

- ½ block of extra firm tofu

- 2 teaspoons of soy sauce

- 3 teaspoons of sesame oil

- 2 celery stalks, diced

- 1 carrot, diced into small pieces

- 1 small white or yellow onion, diced

- ½ cup of green peas

- ½ cup of corn

- ½ cup of spinach, cooked and finely diced

- 2-3 tablespoons of olive oil

Add sesame seed oil in a large skillet on high and add the tofu. Pan sear for 1-2 minutes on each side, to sear each side of the tofu cubes, then remove from the heat and transfer onto a plate. Return the skillet to the stove and heat on medium with olive oil and toss in the celery, onion, carrots, and spinach. Simmer for another 2-3 minutes, then add in the cooked rice and pour in the soy sauce. Cook for 5 minutes until all rice is coated and mixed with the other ingredients. Add in the peas, corn, and tofu. Serve in bowls.

Snacks: Kale Chips

Vegetable chips, including varieties of kale chips in various flavors, tend to be expensive. They have grown in popularity because of kale's reputation as a healthy vegetable, and how creating a tasty snack helps encourage people to enjoy it.

- 1 bunch of kale, rinsed, dried and sliced into one-inch pieces, and stems removed

- 3 tablespoons of melted coconut oil or olive oil

- ½ tablespoon of sea salt

Wash and pat dry the kale before slicing and removing the stems. Coat lightly in oil and arrange on a large baking tray. Sprinkle the sea salt evenly and bake for 8-10 minutes on 375 degrees. Remove to cool for five minutes, then serve.

Dinner: Broccoli and Cheese Casserole

Comfort food can be healthy, as well as tasty, and this dish is proof. Cheese is layered with sliced broccoli and cauliflower florets in a casserole dish that's baked in the oven.

- 2 cups of sliced broccoli florets

- 2 cups of sliced cauliflower florets

- ¾ cups of mozzarella cheese

- ¾ cups of shredded cheddar

- ½ cup of gouda cheese

- 2 tablespoons of butter

- 2 teaspoons of almond flour

- 3 teaspoons of parmesan cheese

- 4 tablespoons skim milk

Melt 2 tablespoons of butter in a microwave for 30 seconds, then mix with milk, and shredded cheese. Combine both the broccoli and cauliflower florets together, and blend with the cheese, milk, and butter. Pour into a medium baking dish or casserole pan coated with olive oil or butter. Pour vegetables in and leave a handful of shredded cheese for the top. With a fork, mix the paprika, black pepper, and almond flour together in a small bowl, then sprinkle evenly over the casserole. Bake in the oven for approximately 30-40 minutes at 350 degrees.

3.1.5 Friday

Breakfast: Poached Eggs with Arugula on Rye

Protein, iron, and fiber are three major nutrients you'll be served in this deliciously simple breakfast dish. Arugula, like kale and spinach, is high in iron, calcium, and fiber and makes a great addition to soup, salad, or sandwich. Arugula also enhances the flavor of your first meal of the day.

- 2 slices of rye bread

- 2 eggs

- ½ cup of feta cheese or shredded gouda

- 1 cup of fresh arugula, sliced

- Dash of black pepper

- 3 cups of water

- 1 teaspoon of olive oil

- 2 teaspoons of parmesan cheese

- 1 teaspoon of paprika

Boil water in a large cooking pot, then adds a dash of salt. Once boiling, add in each egg, one at a time, by cracking them open and gently dropping the yolk and while into the water. Cook on high heat for the other 10 minutes, until eggs are cooked. In the meantime, toast two slices of rye. Combine parmesan cheese, olive oil, and paprika to create a pesto and spread this on each slice of bread. Layer with fresh arugula and add one poached egg on top of each. Sprinkle with black pepper and paprika, then serve.

Lunch: Salmon Wrap with Arugula and Sprouts

This wrap is quick and easy to assemble with leftover baked salmon. In a pinch, cook a small salmon steak on the stovetop with garlic, butter, and olive oil, to prepare this tasty, protein and nutrient-rich lunch.

- 1 small or medium salmon steak (or the equivalent size)

- 4 slices of onion rings

- 2 teaspoons of freshly squeezed lemon

- ½ tablespoon of dried or fresh dill

- Dash of chili pepper

- ½ teaspoon of black pepper

- I read pepper, sliced lengthwise

- Dash of sea salt

- 1 large tortilla shell

Heat the skillet to prepare the salmon and cook a small or medium-sized salmon steak with olive oil until well done. Sprinkle with salt, add pepper, and dill. Simmer the onion rings and sliced peppers for 2-3 minutes. In the center of the tortilla, add the salmon, vegetables, and spices. Squeeze a small dash of lemon, then wrap and serve.

Snacks: Roasted Pinenut Hummus

Pinenuts are a great source of protein and healthy fats. They blend well with chickpeas, tahini, and lemon to create a thick and tasty dip. To soften pinenuts, soak them in water overnight, and blend them with the basic hummus ingredients to make this delicious snack, which can be enjoyed with fresh vegetables, whole-grain crackers, or as a spread in a wrap or sandwich.

- ¼ cup of pinenuts

- ½ cup of water

- 1 can of chickpeas

- 1 cup of tahini butter

- ½ teaspoon of sea salt

- 1/8 cup of fresh lemon juice

- 1 teaspoon of cumin powder

- Dash of black pepper

Soak the raw pinenuts in water to soften them. Two hours or overnight in the refrigerator is ideal. Drain both the pinenuts and cooked or canned chickpeas, and combine them in a blender, along with the remaining ingredients. Blend until smooth, and top with paprika or a handful of raw pinenuts, then serve.

Dinner: Macaroni and Cheese Bake

A simple, filling dish that is often considered comfort food can be slightly upgraded to a healthier version, by combining whole-grain noodles with zucchini spirals and feta cheese mixed with two or three cheese options of your choice. The low carb version of this dish can simply be an assortment of your favorite vegetables mixed with some whole grain or gluten-free noodles, or simply on their own.

- 2 cups of macaroni noodles (gluten-free and/or low carb is recommended)

- 2 cups of sliced vegetables (broccoli, spinach, cauliflower is good options)

- 3 cups of shredded cheese

- 2 tablespoons of butter, melted at room temperature

- 2 teaspoons of sea salt

In a medium or small baking dish, lightly coat with butter and set aside. Boil 3-4 cups of water, and add sea salt, then the macaroni noodles. Cook until tender, then remove to drain and rinse in a colander. Set aside and mix with the vegetables and toss in the shredded cheese. Scoop the ingredients into the casserole dish to bake for approximately 30-35 minutes in the oven at 350 degrees until tender and cheese are melted, then serve.

3.1.6 Saturday

Breakfast: Chia Seed Granola on Greek Yogurt

This is a great way to get all the protein and nutrients you need for breakfast. The chia seeds and granola offer a healthy dose of energy in the morning, along with the protein and calcium contained in the yogurt.

- ¼ cup of chia seeds

- 2 cups of plain, Greek yogurt

- ½ cup of granola

- 2 teaspoons of honey or maple syrup

In a jar, combine the yogurt and sweetener, and gently mix in the chia seeds. Top with granola and add extra honey or maple syrup on top. As an additional option, sprinkle crushed almonds or shredded coconut.

Lunch: Pumpkin Risotto

This is a tasty rice dish that combines the distinct flavor of pumpkin with cheese in a dish that can be enjoyed as a meal on its own, or as aside.

- 1 cup of pureed pumpkin

- 3 cups of vegetable broth

- 1 ½ cups of rice (uncooked)

- 1 teaspoon of thyme

- ½ tablespoon of black pepper

- ½ cup of shredded parmesan

- 1 teaspoon of nutmeg

Boil the vegetable broth in a cooking pot and stir in the pumpkin puree. Lower the heat to high-medium, and pour in the rice, cover, and cook. Add the thyme, black pepper, and nutmeg, then stir, cover again and cook until rice is ready. Serve in bowls topped with grated parmesan cheese. Crumbled feta or goat cheese is another option.

Snacks: Tahini Maple Cookies

These are tasty as a snack or light dessert. Due to the protein content, they can be enjoyed with coffee or tea at breakfast as well.

- 1 cup of tahini butter

- Cup almond flour

- 2 teaspoons maple syrup

- 1 teaspoon of sesame seeds

Combine the tahini, flour, and maple syrup in a bowl to mix. Form dough into small balls then flattens with a fork on the lined baking tray. Sprinkle sesame seeds on each cookie, then bake at 375 degrees for approximately 12 minutes or until lightly golden.

Dinner: Roast Chicken Dinner

A meal that can often a while to roast need not take too many ingredients or items to prepare ahead. Since the first week focuses mostly on vegan and vegetarian meals, this can be skipped for another meal without meat, or prepared for the following week's recipes.

- 1 whole chicken

- 3 onions

- 4-5 cloves of garlic

Prepare the chicken by washing and removing the giblets. Add in the garlic cliffs and onions, chopped in quarters. Preheat the oven to 350 degrees, and cook for 3-4 hours, depending on how long it is needed, based on the size of the chicken. Serve with other sides, or use for other neals in this meal plan.

3.1.7 Sunday, the "Meatless" Day

Breakfast: Vegetable Omelet

Adding a few tasty vegetables to an omelet is an ideal way to get a few exits vitamins for breakfast.

- 3 eggs

- ½ cup of spinach

- 1 teaspoon of paprika

- ¼ cup of diced red pepper

- 1 teaspoon black pepper

Heat the skillet on medium with olive oil. In a medium bowl, combine three eggs and add in the diced vegetables. Stir in the paprika and black pepper. Pour in the mixture on fry lightly on both sides, then remove and serve. Fold and add cheese, if desired: cheddar, mozzarella, and/or feta cheese are all good options.

Lunch: Veggie Pasta

This meal is created with spiral noodles, zucchini, and sweet potato, both of which resemble noodles when cutting into spiral shapes. These are served raw with a lightly flavored tomato sauce.

- 2 cups of pureed tomatoes

- 1 teaspoon of oregano

- ½ tablespoon of black pepper

- Dash of salt

- 2 cups of raw zucchini and/or sweet potato noodles

Combine the pureed tomatoes with spices in a medium cooking pot, and heat on medium, stirring frequently. Pour over a bed of raw vegetable noodles. Add your choice of cheese on top.

Snacks: Fava Bean Dip

If you enjoy hummus and other bean-based dips, you may want to try creating this mild, slightly sweet, fava bean. Before adding fava beans to create this dip, soak them overnight in a cooking pot or container in the refrigerator, then drain, and cook until tender.

- 2 cups of cooked fava beans

- 1/8 cups of white wine vinegar

- 2 cloves of garlic, crushed

- 1 teaspoon of sea salt

- 1 tablespoon of lemon juice

- ¼ cup of olive oil

Mix the above ingredients in a blender and process until smooth. If desired, add in crushed walnuts or pecans for more flavor, and serve.

Dinner: Vegan Chili

This is an excellent meal for winter months and to fill up quickly with a small portion of food. Chili is also a great option for leftovers and usually lasts for several weeks in the refrigerator.

- 1 ½ cups of kidney beans

- 1 ½ cups of chickpeas

- 1 ½ cups of pinto beans

- 1 ½ cups of black beans

- 2 cups of diced tomatoes

- 3 tablespoons of tomato paste

- 1 tablespoon of oregano

- 2 teaspoons of chili powder

- 1 teaspoon of black pepper

- 5 cloves of garlic, crushed

- 1 cup of diced onion

- 1 cup of diced green pepper

To prepare dry beans: soak overnight in water, then drain the following morning. This will soften and prepare for cooking.

In a medium skillet, heat the olive oil and garlic for 1-2 minutes, then add in black pepper, chili pepper, and oregano. Add in the green pepper and onion, and continue to saute for 6-7 minutes. Transfer to a large cooking pot and combine with two cups of diced tomatoes, and heat on medium. Add the tomato paste, then stir thoroughly. Combine the beans (ensure they have been previously soaked and prepared beforehand before mixing). Stew and continually cook on medium until all the ingredients are thoroughly mixed. Lower the heat, then simmer for two hours. Add more spice and seasoning as desired, and taste test, to ensure the spice level is adequate. Serve with rye bread or as aside.

Chapter 4: Second Week healthy Meal Prep

4.1.1 Monday

In the second week of the meal plan, the focus moves from vegan and vegetarian eating to low carb foods. These recipes are suitable for a ketogenic diet or low carb meal plan and include ingredients high in healthy fats and moderate levels of protein while reducing carbohydrates. Fiber is common in most of these meals. If you noticed some weight loss during the first week of the meal plan, you'll see more of a difference following a week of low carb eating. Many people implement a long-term diet comprised of carb restrictions to achieve and maintain their ideal weight.

While a keto or low carb diet often includes red meat and sometimes, fried foods, it's not recommended for healthy eating or as a long term option. Small amounts of lean meat can be enjoyed in a low carb diet as a baked or roasted option. The best options for meat include poultry and seafood. Tofu and tempeh can be used in place of meat for vegan and vegetarian diets.

While some of the recipes in this week include some meat and moderate carbs options, there are substitutes listed available, so that either option can be created in the future, following the three-week plan. Even if you're not considering a plant-based diet, it's a good idea to become familiar with vegan and vegetarian meals, as they will provide a lot of nutrients and support a healthy lifestyle. You'll notice a "meat-free" Sunday, which is a sample of how you might organize all your meals to omit the meat, just for one day. This can be done for a longer time frame as well.

To replace chicken, salmon, and/or other meats or eggs contained in these recipes, add baked tofu or tempeh as a replacement. Roast chicken is included to prepare ahead for the following week, and this can be done similarly with tofu and tempeh, by marinating in the refrigerator for two hours or overnight, then baking in the oven for 20-30 minutes.

Breakfast: Greek Yogurt Parfait

A perfect breakfast that requires little or no time to create, the yogurt parfait consists of three layers:

- The bottom layer consists of chia seeds, oats, hemp hearts and/or flax seeds

- The second layer is full fat or low fat (no sugar) Greek or Icelandic yogurt.

- The third layer is where the topping is added: dark chocolate chips, shredded coconut, dried berries, sliced almonds and your choice of sweetener (maple syrup or honey)

Assemble the three layers and enjoy as a dessert or breakfast. While most of the meals in this plan are prepared for the week, this meal can be assembled minutes before eating or the night before. If not, all the ingredients are available, add any of the ingredients above, and/or a combination of other nuts, seeds, and toppings as desired.

Lunch: Avocado, Chicken and Almond Salad

A satisfying, filling meal on its own, avocado, chicken, and almond contains many of the daily nutrient requirements you'll need in just one meal. This dish is comprised of several "leftover" ingredients, such as roast chicken and cooked quinoa.

- 2 cups of chopped, cooked chicken

- 1 large avocado, sliced

- 2 cups of shredded spinach, kale or lettuce, raw

- 1 cup of sliced almonds

- 3 teaspoons of olive oil

- 2 teaspoons of lime juice

Mix the chicken, greens (your choice of lettuce, kale, or spinach) and almonds together in a large salad bowl. Blend the olive oil and lime juice in a small bowl, then mix into the salad and serve with sliced avocado on top. Sprinkle with black pepper and paprika (optional).

Snacks: Homemade Eggnog

During the holidays, this is an enjoyable drink, though it can be made any time of year, and with a healthier twist.

- 1 teaspoon of nutmeg

- 1 ½ cups of coconut milk

- 1 teaspoon of cinnamon

- ½ cup of cashew nuts

- 2 tablespoons of maple syrup

- 1/8 cup of water

To soften and prepare the cashews, soak them overnight or for a minimum of two hours. Add the soaked cashews and the rest of the ingredients into a food processor, then pulse until smooth. Chill in the refrigerator and serve cold. Garnish with a light dusting of nutmeg or cinnamon.

Dinner: Eggplant Parmesan

A warm and satisfying meal, baked eggplant is a delicious option to add to a meal or enjoy as a main feature.

- 1 medium or large eggplant, sliced into disks

- 1 cup of parmesan cheese

- Sea salt (for preparing the eggplant)

- 1 cup of pureed tomatoes

- 2 teaspoons of oregano

- 1 ½ teaspoon of black pepper

- 2 teaspoons of chili powder

- Dash of salt

Prepare each slice of eggplant by lightly coating in sea salt, then set in a colander for 2p minutes. Rinse, then lightly coat in olive oil, and add to a prepared baking tray. Pour a light cover of pureed tomatoes and sprinkle with parmesan cheese. Bake for 35-40 minutes at 350 degrees, then serve. Eggplant parmesan is best served with pasta or on a bun as a hot sandwich.

4.1.2 Tuesday

Breakfast: Yogurt, Mango and Raspberries

A simple breakfast with protein, calcium, and fiber.

- 2 cups of Greek yogurt (plain, unsweetened)

- 1 cup of fresh berries

- 2 teaspoons of maple syrup or honey

In a small or medium bowl, stir in the honey or maple syrup with the plain yogurt, then top with berries and serve.

Lunch: Waldorf Salad

This is an easy version of a popular salad that combines boiled eggs with lettuce and vegetables. Cherry tomatoes, lettuce, sprouts, and other greens can be added to this dish, along with a light balsamic vinegar dressing, topped with boiled eggs.

- 2 boiled eggs

- 2 cups of shredded lettuce

- ½ cup of sliced cherry tomatoes

- ½ cup of shredded cheese

- 2 tablespoons of olive oil

- 3 teaspoons of lemon juice

- ½ tablespoon of rosemary (dried)

Whisk together the olive oil, rosemary, and lemon juice in a small bowl then set aside. Add the lettuce, cherry tomatoes to a bowl and toss in the salad dressing, then top with two boiled eggs, sliced in half and sprinkled with shredded cheese.

Snacks: Raspberry and Banana Smoothie

This smoothie is easily made with yogurt, milk, raspberries, and a banana. It's a great snack or breakfast option, due to the amount of energy and nutrients.

- ½ cup of Greek yogurt

- 1 ripe banana

- 2 cups of non-dairy milk (coconut or almond)

- 1 cup of fresh or frozen berries

- 2 teaspoons of low carb sweetener

Mix all ingredients into a blender, and pulse until smooth. If berries are not frozen, serve over ice, or add a couple of ice cubes to the blender before mixing.

Dinner: Garlic Shrimp with Rice and Spinach

A handful of small shrimp in the freezer and leftover frozen or cooked spinach are two excellent ingredients to combine into a tasty rice dish.

- 1-2 cups of mini or small shrimp

- 2 ½ teaspoons of olive oil

- 3 cloves of garlic, crushed

- 1 cup of rice (uncooked)

- 1 cup of frozen or cooked spinach

- 2 tablespoons of butter

Defrost the spinach, if frozen, in the microwave, then heat the skillet and add in the shrimp with the olive oil. Saute for 3-4 minutes, then add in the spinach and garlic. In a medium cooking pot, boil two cups of water and add in the rice and a dash of sea salt. Reduce the water and rice to low, then cook with a cover until tender. Once the rice is done, drain and fold into the sautéed shrimp, garlic and spinach with the two tablespoons of butter, stirring to coat the rice. Cook for 4-5 minutes, then serves in bowls. This dish makes 4-6 servings.

4.1.3 Wednesday

Breakfast: Poached Eggs in Tomato Sauce

An ideal start for breakfast or brunch, this skillet dish provides a tasty tomato sauce base with herbs and spices. The eggs are poached inside, then topped with feta cheese.

- 2 cups of tomato sauce (or pureed tomatoes)

- 2 teaspoons of cumin seeds

- ½ tablespoon of black pepper

- 2 cloves of garlic, crushed

- 1 teaspoon of chili pepper

- 2 teaspoons of diced onion

- Fresh parsley

- ¼ cup of feta cheese

- 2 eggs

Heat a skillet medium heat with olive oil, then2 table add the cumin seeds, garlic, black pepper, chili pepper, and diced onion. Sautee for 1-2 minutes, then pour in the tomato sauce. Continue to simmer and add more sauce or ¼ can of water, as needed. Ensure all the ingredients are well mixed, then add one egg at a time. Poach the eggs for 5-6 minutes or until slightly hardened, with soft yolks. Serve from the skillet with toast and avocado.

Lunch: Toasted Red Pepper, Feta Cheese, and Basil Sandwich

This is a quick lunch idea that can be prepared earlier in the day for later and reheated or served cold. The red pepper is lightly roasted in the oven or skillet, and the basil leaves are added fresh, along with the feta cheese.

- 1 whole baked or lightly sautéed red pepper, sliced lengthwise

- 2 slices of rye bread

- ½ cup of crumbled feta cheese

- 2-4 fresh basil leaves

Toast both slices of rye and top with feta, basil, and roasted or sautéed red peppers, then serve.

Snacks: Green Tea Pudding

Matcha green tea powder is combined with silken tofu, sweetener, and a small amount of coconut cream to blend. These are combined in a blender to create a bake-free, raw dessert with a lot of health benefits: green tea is high in antioxidants, while tofu is rich in protein, fiber, and calcium.

- 2 cups of silken tofu

- 3 tablespoons of green tea powder

- 3 teaspoons of natural sweetener

- ½ tablespoon of coconut cream

Blend all the ingredients and pulse for 40-50 seconds in a food processor, or until smooth. Serve in bowls. Top with fruit or sliced banana

Dinner: Roast Turkey with Vegetable Stuffing

Roasting a turkey can take several hours, though it is worthwhile, as it provides for several meal options and servings. Leftover turkey makes excellent options for soup and sandwiches.

- 1 medium-sized turkey

- 3 cups of chopped vegetables

- 1 cup of cooked rice

- ¼ cup of water

- 1 ½ cups of cranberries

- 2 teaspoons of dried sage

- 1 ½ teaspoon of thyme

- 1 ½ teaspoon of tarragon

- 1 teaspoon of rosemary

Defrost the turkey, if frozen, and prepare the oven by preheating to 375 degrees. Wash and rinse the turkey, then remove the giblets. To prepare the stuffing, cook the rice by coiling two cups of water with a dash of salt. Boil the water, then set aside to cool. Combine with chopped vegetables. Any variety can be used, such as celery, broccoli, carrots, mushrooms, and onions. Mix in the spices and cranberries then stuff the turkey. Bake in a large pan for 2-3 hours and continue to baste and monitor the progress. Serve the turkey on its own, or with side dishes.

4.1.4 Thursday

Breakfast: Portobello Eggs Benedict

A fulfilling and rich meal, adding portobello mushrooms adds more fiber and nutrients, and can take the place of bread or English muffins. Asparagus or other vegetables can be used to boost the nutrient level of this dish, with added texture and flavor.

- 2 portobello mushroom caps

- 2 eggs

- 1 package of Hollandaise sauce

- 1 teaspoon of black pepper

- 3 tablespoons of olive oil

- Dash of sea salt

- 6 asparagus spears, sliced 3-4 inches long

Heat a skillet on medium and add both portobello mushroom caps. On the side of the skillet, leave some space to saute the asparagus. In a medium cooking pot, add three cups of water and heat until boiling. Drop-in two eggs, one at a time, and cook until ready.

Saute the portobello mushrooms on both sides until well cooked, then remove from heat. Prepare the Hollandaise sauce, as per the directions on the package. Serve with portobello mushrooms topped with asparagus, then one poached egg per mushroom, and top with Hollandaise sauce and black pepper.

Lunch: Turkey Egg Drop Soup

Leftover turkey is ideal for this dish, which is combined with light rice noodles and egg. Additional ingredients suggested are green beans, celery, carrots, spinach, and broccoli. Other vegetables leftover from a previous meal may also be added.

- 2 cups of cooked turkey

- 4-5 cups of vegetable or chicken broth (or make turkey broth by boiling the bones in a large cooking pot, and letting it stand 20-24 hours).

- 2 eggs

- 1 ½ cups of rice noodles

- ½ tablespoon of black pepper

- 2 teaspoons of sea salt

- 2 teaspoons of thyme

- 1 teaspoon of poultry spice

- 1-2 cups of leftover or freshly sliced vegetables

Boil the water with added sea salt. Stir in the spices, then drop one egg in at a time, and gently stir. Add in turkey and noodles, then stir in the vegetables. Cook until noodles and vegetables are tender, then serve. This dish makes 3-4 servings.

Snacks: Cucumber, Cream Cheese and Salmon Bites

This snack can be enjoyed at home on a platter, or on the go. Smoked or baked salmon is an ideal topping for this treat.

- 1 large cucumber, sliced into disks

- 1 cup of plain cream cheese (low fat)

- 1 package of smoked salmon, sliced into one- or two-inch pieces, or baked salmon separated into similar sized portions

- 2 teaspoons of capers

- Dash of black pepper

Add cream cheese to each cucumber slice, then top with salmon. Add a couple of capers and sprinkle with black pepper. Serve on a platter, and add toothpicks if necessary, to keep the toppings together.

Dinner: Mashed Yams with Sliced Turkey

Using the leftover turkey or chicken is ideal as a side to a fresh batch of mashed yams. If desired, replace turkey with another leftover side, such as tofu, squash, or eggplant.

- 3 large yams

- 2 cloves of garlic, crushed

- 2 tablespoons of butter

- ¼ cup of cream

Boil four cups of water with a dash of sea salt. Peel and slice the yams into small, one-inch pieces and add to the water. Cook on high for ten minutes, then reduce to medium and cook until tender. Drain, then add the garlic, butter, and cream. Mash and serve with sliced, oven-baked turkey or another side.

4.1.5 Friday

Breakfast: Breakfast Salad

Scrambled eggs work well as a base for a morning salad of fresh vegetables. This combination is perfect to start your day with fresh vitamins and protein for energy.

- 3 eggs

- 1 cucumber, diced

- 2 small tomatoes, diced

- ¼ cup of black olives, sliced

- ½ red onion, diced

- 1 tablespoon of mayonnaise

- 2 teaspoons of lemon or lime juice

- 1 ½ teaspoon of black pepper

Heat a skillet on medium and scramble the eggs until they are done. Add to the base of a medium bowl. In a separate bowl, the vegetables and salad dressing options, and mix thoroughly. Pour on top of the eggs, and add a dash more black pepper, then serve.

Lunch: Egg Salad Sandwich

Rye or whole grain bread is a great base for this sandwich, which can be enjoyed with two slices, or open-faced.

- 2 boiled eggs

- 1 teaspoon of dill

- ½ tablespoon of black pepper

- 1 tablespoon of mayonnaise

- ½ teaspoon of lemon or lime juice

- Dash of chili pepper flakes

- ½ teaspoon of butter

- ½ teaspoon of paprika

- 2 slices of rye or whole-grain bread

In a small bowl, mash the boiled eggs (ensure they have cooled before including them), then add in the spices, mayonnaise, and lemon or lime juice. Mix thoroughly and serve on top of the bread (raw or toasted, with butter).

Snacks: Green Tea Smoothie

- 2 tablespoons of green tea matcha powder

- 1 tablespoon of low carb sweetener

- 2 ¼ cups of almond milk

- 1 banana

Blend all the above ingredients until smooth, then serve on ice.

Dinner: Baked Tofu

This is a simple, easy dish to create using one block of tofu, sesame oil, and soy sauce.

- 1 block of extra firm tofu

- ¼ cups of soy sauce

- ¼ cup of sesame oil

Mix soy sauce and sesame oil in a small bowl. Drain and rinse the tofu, and slice into cubes. Marinate in the oil and soy sauce mix and refrigerate for two hours.
Prepare a small baking dish for a preheated oven at 350 degrees. Drain the tofu and add to the dish, baking for

15-20 minutes, or until browned and slightly crispy around the edges. Remove and serve.

4.1.6 Saturday

Breakfast: Kefir and Peach Smoothie

Kefir is like yogurt, only with more probiotics and made with a stronger fermentation process. It's a great foundation for smoothies due to its slightly thinner consistency and mixes well with fruits.

- 2 fresh peaches, cored and sliced

- 2 cups of kefir

- ½ cup of coconut milk

Combine the ingredients and blend for 30 seconds, or until smooth.

Lunch: Lentil Soup

- 1 cup of lentils (red)

- 4 cups of vegetable broth

- 1 carrot, diced

- 3 small potatoes, diced into small cubes

- 3 teaspoons of cumin

- 3 teaspoons of turmeric

- Dash of black pepper

- Dash of chili powder

In a medium or large cooking pot, bring the four cups of broth to boil, and add in the lentils and spices. Add the carrots and potatoes, then cook on medium until all ingredients are tender, then serve.

Snacks: Sautéed Plantain

Plantain is a tasty and high energy fruit that can be added to desserts or more commonly enjoyed as chips. In this recipe, plantain is lightly sautéed on the skillet with cinnamon.

- 1 large plantain, sliced into disks

- 2 tablespoons of cinnamon

- 1 teaspoon of low carb sweetener

Prepare a skillet by heating on medium, and add the olive oil. Combine the plantain and lightly coat with the cinnamon and low carb sweetener (raw sugar can also be used). Fry gently on medium until lightly browned and soft, then serve with cream.

Dinner: Sweet and Sour Tempeh

To prepare tempeh, marinate in a combination of soy sauce, 2 tablespoons of orange or berry marmalade and 2 tablespoons of sesame oil.

- 1 block of tempeh (unflavored)

- 2 tablespoons of sesame oil

- 2 tablespoons of marmalade (berry or orange flavor)

- ¼ cup of soy sauce

Drain and rinse the tempeh and marinade in the combination of the ingredients above. Place the marinated tempeh in the center of a preheated oven and bake for 25-30 minutes at 375 degrees, then slice and serve.

4.1.7 Sunday

Breakfast: Crepes with Fruit

Crepes are light, smooth-textured, and easy to make. They are often filled with sugary ingredients, though fortunately, they can be created in a low carb, the natural version that retains the same taste.

- 1 ¼ cups of almond flour

- 1 cup of tapioca flour

- 1 ½ teaspoon of vanilla extract

- 1 cup of coconut milk

- 1 cup of fresh berries (any variety or mix)

- 1 sliced peach or mango

Prepare a skillet on medium heat, then add two teaspoons of olive oil. Mix the tapioca and almond flour, then combine with the vanilla extract and coconut milk. Whisk until a thin batter is formed. Pour 4-5 inch-sized portions on the skillet and heat for 1 or 2 minutes on both sides until golden, then remove from the stovetop and serve with fresh fruit.

Lunch: Carrot Ginger Soup

Ideal for a cold, carrot ginger soup is both a strong dose of antioxidants and vitamins in one dish. It's thick, warming soup that can be enjoyed as a meal on its own, or as a side dish or appetizer.

- 2 carrots, diced

- 1 tablespoon of ground ginger

- 2 cups of vegetable broth

- 1 teaspoon of sea salt

- 2 ½ teaspoons of black pepper

- 1 small onion, diced

Bring two cups of vegetable broth to boil and add in the carrots and ginger in a large pot. Cook on medium until tender, then add the black pepper, sea salt, and onion. Simmer for another 15-20 minutes on low-medium. Remove and cool the soup for 10-15 minutes, then blend the mixture in batches, and return to the stovetop to reheat. Serve with a sprinkle of fresh dill or cilantro.

Snacks: Almonds and Dried Fruit

If you are a fan of trail mix and looking for healthy snacks, this is a great idea. Almonds are best as roasted or raw, without salt, and dried fruit can vary from apricots and prunes to berries and raisins. Dried coconut chips and apple chips are also great options to add and can often be found around the produce or bulk section of the grocery store.

- ¾ cups of apricots

- ½ cups of dried cherries

- 1 cup of raw or lightly roasted almonds

- ½ cup of coconut slices

- ½ cup of raisins

- ½ cup of cashews or peanuts (optional)

Combine the ingredients into a bowl and determine whether to add more. For a sweeter taste, add more dried cherries and apricots.

Dinner: Chicken and Quinoa Salad with Fruit

Baked chicken or prepared on the skillet is done prior to creating this dish. Roast chicken from a previous meal is another good option, and only a small amount is needed: one cup at the most. The remaining ingredients include quinoa cooked in a chicken broth with a topping of dried fruits and nuts.

- 1 cup of cooked chicken

- 1 cup of quinoa, uncooked

- 2 cups of chicken broth

- 1 teaspoon of thyme

- ½ cup of crushed walnuts and/or pecans

- ½ cup of dried berries

Bring the two cups of broth to boil, then add in the quinoa, then lower to medium. Cook, as covered under grains, are tender, then remove and mix with cooked chicken. Serve in a bowl and top with nuts and berries.

Chapter 5: Third Week Healthy Meal Prep

5.1.1 Monday

During the final week of the three-week healthy meal plan, many of the recipes continue as the previous weeks, with a focus on using easy to find and healthy ingredients, which make the day-to-day and advance planning helpful. The following grocery items, in addition, the previous two weeks, should be considered:

- Fresh pineapples, mangos, peaches, apples, pears, and other fruits

- Frozen berries and other fruits

- Coconut milk is a good staple, and/or almond milk

- Always have chicken, lean meat and/or tofu and tempeh on hand to prepare a variety of quick and easy meals

- An assortment of nuts and seeds

- Rice (long grain and/or basmati)

- Quinoa

- Rye bread and/or whole-grain bread (if you buy in advance, freeze any extra to avoid spoilage, and use one loaf at a time)

- Bananas and avocados are great to have on hand at all times.

- Cheese (goat cheese, such as feta, is a good option). Make sure to choose from natural, organic cheese and avoid chemically processed products. If possible, buy from local farmers and cheese artisans.

Breakfast: Coconut, Pineapple, and Banana Protein Milkshake

- 2 cups of coconut milk

- 1 cup of sliced pineapples (frozen or fresh)

- 2 ¼ cups of coconut milk

- 1 ripe banana

- 2 teaspoons of vanilla protein powder

Combine the ingredients into a blender and pulse for 30 seconds or until smooth.

Lunch: Sautéed Kale with Apricots and Walnuts

An easy stovetop dish, this recipe combines lightly sautéed kale and olive oil with the sweet flavor of apricots and nutty taste of walnuts for a tasty, balanced meal.

- 2 cups of thinly sliced or grated kale (stems removed)

- 1 cup of dried apricots, sliced in half or quarters

- ½ cup of crushed walnuts

Heat a skillet on medium and toss in the sliced kale and simmer for 5-6 minutes. Remove and serve topped with the apricots and walnuts. If desired, kale can be served raw and with a salad dressing as follows:

- ½ tablespoon of orange juice

- 2 teaspoons of olive or coconut oil

- 1 teaspoon of white wine vinegar

Snacks: Crushed Strawberries Over Ice

This is an easy drink to make and serves as a refreshing snack in place of soda or candy. Naturally sweet and tart, strawberries contain a lot of antioxidants, vitamin C, and fiber. They work well mixed with other berries, or on their own.

- 1 cup of frozen or fresh strawberries

- ½ cup of water

- ½ cup of ice

- 2 teaspoons of low carb sweetener or raw sugar (optional)

Combine the strawberries, water, and ice into the blender and pulse for 40-50 seconds. If the results are not as smooth as desired, add another two tablespoons of water, then blend and serve   Alternatively, if frozen strawberries are used instead of fresh, add water and sweetener only, and omit the ice.

Variations on this recipe include adding coconut cream or yogurt in place of water, then serving over ice.

Dinner: Chicken and Cabbage Casserole

This meal is ideal for leftover roast chicken and vegetables. Cabbage is added to this dish for its nutrients and texture. It contains a mellow taste that blends well with other ingredients.

- 2 ¼ cups of chopped, cooked chicken (if the chicken isn't already cooked, heat on the skillet and sauté with olive oil and your choice of seasoning and spices)

- 2 cups of shredded cabbage

- ½ small onion, diced

- 2 sliced carrots

- 1 sliced celery stalk

- ½ cup of chicken broth

- Dash of sea salt

- ½ tablespoon of black pepper

- 1/8 cups of whole wheat flour

- 2 teaspoons of soy sauce

Lightly coat a casserole dish in olive oil. Combine the chicken pieces with shredded cabbage in a large bowl, then mix in the remaining vegetables. Stir until unevenly mixed. In a second bowl, stir the flour and broth with soy sauce, then add to the vegetable and chicken mix. Pour in the casserole, add the spices, and bake at 325 degrees for 35-45 minutes.

5.1.2 Tuesday

Breakfast: Chia Seed Yogurt Parfait

Chia seeds are perfect as an ingredient or topping, as they contain many nutrients in one serving. Yogurt is a tasty and nutritious breakfast food, and because it is fermented, it provides a good boost of probiotics that benefit your gut health.

- 2 cups of plain, unsweetened yogurt (Greek yogurt is recommended)

- 2-3 tablespoons of low carb syrup, honey or maple syrup

- ½ cup of chia seeds

- 2 tablespoons of natural marmalade or berry jam (unsweetened or natural sweetener preferred)

Combine the yogurt and chia seeds, then stir in the sweetener, followed by the jam or marmalade, creating a "swirl" pattern, then serve.

Lunch: Rice Pilaf With Pistachios and Cherries

Rice pilaf is a tasty way to enjoy rice in many different flavors. This recipe adds the dynamic of pistachio nuts with the sweetness of dried cherries.   Long grain or basmati rice is recommended, as it is aromatic and works well in a variety of flavorful dishes.

- 3 cups of water

- 1 ½ cups of long grain or basmati rice

- 2 teaspoons of cardamom

- ½ cup of raw, crushed pistachios

- ¼ cup of dried cherries (sweet or tart)

Boil three cups of water in a large cooking pot and add a dash of sea salt. Pour in the rice and cook, covered, on medium-low until tender. Remove to cool, then add the cardamom spice, crushed pistachios, and dried cherries. If dried cherries are unavailable, use cranberries as an alternative.

Snacks: Fruit Salad

If you have a lot of fruit in your kitchen, this is a good sign! It means you include a lot of vitamins, minerals, and fiber in your diet, and while you may have every intention of using them, often, we get too busy and forget some of the foods we have, until it is too late, because they are perishable. With this dish, combine all of the fruit you find in your refrigerator, and enjoy it. A sample of fruit options is listed below.

- 2 peaches, pitted and sliced

- 1 cup of fresh berries (any variety or mix)

- 1 orange, peeled and sliced

- 1 cup of grapes (any variety, preferably without pits)

- 1 kiwi, sliced

- 1 mango (any variety), cored, pitted and sliced

- 1 cup of diced pineapple

Dinner: Turkey and Rice Soup

If you have leftover turkey in the refrigerator or freezer, this soup is an ideal way to use it and create a hearty dinner at the same time. Any rice left from other recipes can be added to this soup, or additional rice can be cooked.

- 4 cups of chicken or turkey broth

- Leftover roast turkey

- 2 teaspoons of sea salt

- 2 cups of cooked rice, or one cup uncooked

- 1 ½ cups of green peas

- 1 ½ cups of corn

Boil the broth in a large pot, then add in the rice, if uncooked. Stir and cover on medium until softened, then add remaining ingredients and cook on medium-low for 30-40 minutes. This recipe provides 4 servings.

5.1.3 Wednesday

Breakfast: Skillet Eggs with Greens

- 1 cup of cooked or frozen spinach

- 1 cup of sliced kale or other greens

- 3 eggs

- 2 tablespoons of olive oil

Add the olive oil and greens to a heated skillet on medium with olive oil. Simmer for 5-6 minutes, then add the eggs to scramble. Simmer for 2-3 minutes and add desired spices, such as paprika, sea salt and/or black pepper, then serve.

Lunch: Asparagus with Toasted Almonds

- 1 bunch of asparagus

- ½ cup of slivered almonds, lightly toasted on the skillet

- Olive oil to cook

- 3 tablespoons of butter

In a medium skillet, heat on medium with olive oil and add in the asparagus. Saute for 8-10 minutes, then remove and top with additional butter and sliced almonds.

Snacks: Sliced Vegetables with Olives and Cheese

This dish is a platter that combines an assortment of the following:

- Black and green olives

- Feta cheese cubes

- Sliced carrots

- Sliced celery

- Fresh berries

- Pickles

- Leftover oven roasted tofu, chicken or turkey

Dinner: Kale Chicken Salad with Roasted Chickpeas

This recipe combines a few leftover options: roasted chicken and lightly roasting chickpeas left from a previous meal. To prepare the chickpeas, roast in an olive oil coated the pan in the oven for ten minutes, then remove. Add to a bowl of sliced kale, and toss in the chicken and chickpeas.

- 2 cups of leftover chicken (cooked, baked)

- 3 cups of thinly sliced kale

- 1 cup of oven-roasted chickpeas

- 1 cup of lemon juice mixed with olive oil and poultry spice (dressing)

Combine the ingredients above, with the roasted chickpeas as the topping, then serve.

5.1.4 Thursday

Breakfast: Protein Pancakes with Banana

These pancakes add an extra layer of protein, with hemp or pumpkin seed powder.

- 2 tablespoons of hemp or pumpkin seed protein powder

- 1 ¼ cups of coconut flour

- 1 ¼ cups of almond flour

- ½ tablespoon of vanilla extract

- 2 cups of coconut milk

- 1 tablespoon of low carb sweetener

- 1 banana

- 2 tablespoons of coconut cream, or more, if desired.

Combine and mix the coconut and almond flour in a large bowl, then add the protein powder. Heat a skillet on medium with olive oil. In the meantime, continue mixing the pancake batter by combining the coconut milk and vanilla extract, and whisking together all ingredients. If the mixture is becoming too thick, add another ¼ cup of almond or coconut milk. Pour the batter into the skillet, then and on each side for 2-3 minutes each. Serve topped with sliced banana and coconut cream.

Lunch: Noodle and Veggie Salad With Sesame Seeds

This is an ideal dish created with leftover sautéed vegetables, spaghetti noodles, and topped with sesame seeds.

- 2 cups of cooked spaghetti

- 2 cups of sautéed vegetables (bell peppers, onions, garlic, etc.)

- 3 teaspoons of sesame seeds

- 4 teaspoons of olive oil

- 1 ½ tablespoon of soy sauce

Heat the olive oil on medium and toss in the cooked spaghetti in a large skillet. Cook with soy sauce for approximately 4-5 minutes, before adding the vegetables. Cook for another 10-15 minutes and serve with sesame seeds as a topping.

Snacks: Mango and Banana Smoothie

- 1 medium mango, pitted, peeled and sliced

- 1 banana

- 2 cups of kefir (unsweetened, unflavored)

- 2 tablespoons of low carb sweetener or syrup

Mix the above ingredients into a blender, then pulse until smooth. If too thick, add ½ cup of almond or coconut milk and mix, then serve.

Dinner: Loaded Baked Potato

This recipe uses a baked potato as a base and builds to create a tasty dinner. To prepare, bake 3-4 large or medium-sized potatoes in the oven for 60-70 minutes (poke with a fork and wrap well in tin foil before baking, for best results). When the potatoes are done, slice open and add the following toppings:

- 1 tablespoon of butter

- 1 cup of shredded cheese (any variety)

- ½ cup of steamed broccoli

- 2 tablespoons of sour cream

- 2 tablespoons of refried black beans

- Black pepper, sea salt, chili pepper as options

- Sautéed bell peppers and/or onions

5.1.5 Friday

Breakfast: Peanut Chocolate Smoothie

Peanut butter is an amazing source of protein and can provide a quick boost in the morning. Combined with dark, natural chocolate, and coconut milk, these ingredients create an excellent breakfast on the go and without fuss. Chocolate almond or soymilk can also be used in place of coconut milk

- 2 cup of coconut milk (almond or soymilk work well)

- 3-4 tablespoons of dark cocoa powder (unsweetened)

- 3 teaspoons of low carb sweetener or maple syrup

- ½ cup of smooth peanut butter (unsweetened, unsalted)

In a blender and mix all the ingredients until smooth, about 30-45 seconds. For a thicker smoothie, add one or half a banana, then serve.

Lunch: Spaghetti and Meat Sauce

Extra-lean ground beef, chicken, or lamb can be easily used to create this dish. Spaghetti noodles that are whole grain and organic are recommended for the best quality and good nutrient value.

- 1 pound of extra-lean ground beef, chicken or lamb

- ¼ cup of parmesan (fresh, grated)

- Dash of black pepper

- 2 cups of pureed tomatoes

- 1 teaspoon of oregano

- 2 garlic cloves, crushed

- ½ onion, diced

- ½ teaspoon of chili powder or cayenne

- 3 teaspoons of olive oil

- 4 cups of water

- ½ or 1 package of spaghetti noodles (whole grain, organic)

Heat olive oil on a skillet at a medium temperature, then add the meat. Cook on medium until well done, then add the onions, garlic, and spices. Simmer at a reduced temperature, until all ingredients are thoroughly mixed and tender. Slowly pour in the pureed tomatoes and stir consistently and gently, creating the meat sauce. Reduce heat to low and simmer.

In a large cooking pot, pour 4 cups of water and a dash of sea salt. Bring to a boil, and add in the spaghetti, divided or broken in half. Cook on medium, covered until all noodles are tender. Drain in a colander, rinse and serve with the meat and tomato sauce. Coat the dish with parmesan cheese.

Snacks: Almond and Avocado Smoothie

Smoothies make excellent snacks because they are quick and easy to create, and both tasty and filling. Almond milk is a good source of protein and healthy fats, which makes it an ideal base for smoothies and drinks in general. Avocados contain lots of fiber and healthy fats and texture that suits many dishes, including milkshakes and smoothies.

- 2 cups of almond milk

- 1 large, ripe avocado, pitted, peeled and sliced

- 2 teaspoons of low carb sweetener, honey or maple syrup

Mix the above ingredients into a blender and pulse until smooth. Serve the smoothie immediately, or transfer to a thermos or portable container and enjoy on the go. For added flavor, add one or two tablespoons of cocoa powder and/or a banana.

Dinner: Baked Zucchini with Pasta Sauce and Parmesan

If you have leftover meat pasta sauce from lunch, this can be used in this recipe, or a new batch can be created, with or without meat. This dish is a simple baked vegetable with a light coating of tomato sauce and parmesan.

- 2 large or medium zucchinis

- 1 cup of tomato puree (or leftover pasta sauce from the lunch recipe)

- ½ cup of parmesan cheese, grated

- Dash of sea salt

- 2 ½ teaspoons of olive oil

Prepare a small or medium-sized prepared baking dish. Brush the dish in olive oil. Slice the zucchini lengthwise and arrange in the dish. Lightly salt and bake for 20-25 minutes at 375 degrees, or until zucchini is tender. Remove and pour the tomato puree or pasta sauce, then place back into the oven, and bake for another 5-6 minutes, then serve topped with parmesan cheese.

5.1.6 Saturday

Breakfast: Skillet Brunch

If you have leftover vegetables from a previous dinner or unused in your refrigerator or freezer, this is the perfect way to use them before they are forgotten. Often, we buy ingredients for various meals, and end up with extra, which risks going to waste. Creating a skillet brunch is one way to use up the vegetables in a breakfast or brunch stir fry. In this dish, eggs are scrambled and added with the leftover or unused ingredients. The list below can be modified to include the vegetables you have in your own kitchen or use the exact items as shown.

- 2 eggs

- Celery, carrots, broccoli, cauliflower, snow peas, (any other vegetables in your refrigerator or freezer)

- ½ tablespoon of soy sauce

- 1 tablespoon of olive oil

Heat a skillet with olive oil, then add the vegetables. Cook for 2-3 minutes, and add in the soy sauce. In a small bowl, whisk two eggs, then add them into the skillet and scramble them to mix with the vegetables. Serve from the skillet or with a fruit salad and/or toast.

Lunch: Baked Apple With Oats and Cinnamon

Baked apples can work as a dessert or lunch, especially since they are healthy and contain some essential nutrients, such as fiber and vitamin C. Combined with oats, they are an excellent source of protein and a healthy dose of energy. Cinnamon is used to flavor this dish instead of sugar or maple syrup. If desired, a little light sweetener can be combined with cinnamon before topping this meal.

- 2 large peeled and cored apples, sliced

- 1 ½ teaspoon of cinnamon

- 3 teaspoons of olive oil

- 1 cup of raw oats

- ½ cup of almond flour

- 1 teaspoon of low carb sweetener or raw sugar

Prepare a medium or small baking dish coated in olive oil. Place the sliced apples on the bottom of the pan, creating a thin layer. Combine the oats and almond flour in a separate bowl. Lightly coat the apples, with the oat and flour mix, then add another layer of apples, and repeat, until there is a final layer of apples on top. Coat with a sprinkling of almond flour and cinnamon (and sweetener, if desired). Bake for 25-30 minutes at 350 degrees, then serve warm with cream or coconut milk ice cream.

Snacks: Mango, Banana, and Berries in Cream

Sometimes, the simplest meals or snacks are the best. Slicing a few select, fresh fruits, and enjoying them with natural dairy or coconut cream is ideal. No sugar or additives are needed, just the raw fruits with cream.

- 1 mango, pitted, peeled and sliced

- 1 banana, sliced in disks

- 1 cup of fresh berries (any type or mix)

- 1 cup of cream (all-natural coconut or dairy cream)

Wash and drain the fruits, then arrange them in a bowl after they are cored, peeled, and sliced. Pour the cream on top evenly, and enjoy immediately. Note: if any or all of the fruits are frozen, defrost them before adding the cream, as this may "freeze" against the fruits if they are not completely thawed.

Dinner: Chicken Fried Rice

An easy and fun recipe to prepare and enjoy, chicken fried rice can be made in small or larger volumes to satisfy a whole family or just one or two people. To prepare the rice, boil two cups of water in a medium cooking pot, and add one teaspoon of sea salt. Pour in one cup of rice and cook, covered, for 10-15 minutes, or until ready. Double the quantity if preparing for a larger group of people, or to provide some leftovers for the following day. For simplicity, one cup of rice is used as the quantity in this recipe, though this can be increased as preferred.

- 1 cup of rice

- 2 cups of water (for the rice)

- 2 chicken breasts (boneless), cut into small, one-inch pieces

- 3 teaspoons of soy sauce

- 1 egg

- 2 stalks of celery

- 1 cup of green peas

- ½ cup of thinly sliced broccoli florets

- ½ cup of baby corn

- 1 cup of fresh or defrosted snow peas

- 3 cloves of crushed garlic

- 1 cup of fresh bean sprouts

- 1 small onion, diced

- 3-4 small white mushrooms, thinly sliced

- 3 teaspoons of sesame seeds (optional)

Prepare a skillet by adding olive oil and heating on medium. Place the small chicken pieces into the pan and cook for approximately 10 or 12 minutes, then add in the soy sauce. Cook chicken until done, add in the garlic, onion, celery, and green peas. Saute for another 5-6 minutes, then add the remaining vegetables, with the mushrooms last. Add in the egg and scramble to mix evenly with the other ingredients. At the very last, fold in the rice until well coated and blended with the vegetables. Reduce heat, then sprinkle in the sesame seeds and serve.

For best results, slice vegetables very small and thin, so they mix well with the rice and other ingredients well.

5.1.7 Sunday

Breakfast: Fried Egg on Rice

Leftover rice doesn't have to be for the next day's lunch or dinner. It can easily be incorporated into the first meal of the day. Fried rice, sticky or steamed rice can be used as a based for poached eggs. Referring to the previous day's menu, there may be some chicken fried rice leftover for this tasty recipe. For a bit more flavor, add the rice in the skillet on medium, with olive oil and soy sauce, then poach the egg and add on top.

- 1-2 cups of cooked rice (steamed or fried, from the day before or just prepared)

- 2 tablespoons of soy sauce

- 3 tablespoons of olive oil

- 2 eggs

- Dash of black pepper

If the rice is steamed, add to a heated skillet with olive oil and soy sauce and simmer for 5-6 minutes. Add 2-3 cups of water in a second cooking pot and boil. Add both eggs in, one at a time, and cook at boiling for 10-

12 minutes, or until done. In the meantime, reduce the skillet temperature to low, then simmer the rice until the eggs are ready. Serve the rice in a bowl or plate and top with the eggs. This dish makes two servings (or one large dish).

For additional ingredients, consider adding one teaspoon of miso paste mixed with ¼ cup of boiling water in the rice. Add fresh parsley and/or sliced green onions. Scrambled tofu is another great choice to add more protein to this meal.

Lunch: Tuna on Rye Bread

Keep your Sunday lunch simple with tuna fish on rye. Baked, flaky tuna is healthy, calcium, and protein-rich fish, with a good source of fats. If rye bread isn't available, consider using any whole grain or sprouted bread, fresh or toasted. Each slice is served open-faced, to maximize the number of toppings and taste.

- Two slices of rye bread

- 2 cups of baked tuna

- 2 teaspoons of mayonnaise

- ½ onion, diced

- 1 teaspoon of chili pepper or cayenne

- Dash of sea salt

- ½ tablespoons of dried dill

- 1 teaspoon of butter

Before preparing the bread, combine the tuna, mayonnaise, onion, chili pepper or cayenne, dill, and salt in a bowl. Add ½ teaspoon of olive oil, if the tuna salad is a bit dry. Toast both slices of rye and butter. Place on a plate and gently add and spread the tuna salad on each, coating evenly. Sprinkle with ground black pepper, then serve.

Snacks: Baked Cauliflower With Hummus

Cauliflower has a distinct flavor that can be enjoyed raw or cooked in a variety of meals or as a snack on its own. In this dish, hummus is prepared as a dip while the cauliflower is roasted in the oven, which takes approximately 15-20 minutes.

- 1 can of chickpeas, drained and rinsed

- 1 cup of tahini (softened, room temperature)

- 1 tablespoon of olive oil, for the hummus, and 2 additional tablespoons for the cauliflower

- 1/8 cups of fresh lemon juice

- ½ tablespoon of cumin

- 1 teaspoon of sea salt

- 1 head of cauliflower

- 1 teaspoon of paprika

Slice the cauliflower into 2-inch pieces, including the stem (if desired) and lightly coat in olive oil. Lightly coat with paprika and sea salt and bake for about 20 minutes in a baking dish at 350 degrees until brown or lightly golden. In the meantime, combine the chickpeas, tahini, lemon juice, cumin, olive oil, sea salt in a blender or food processor, then mix thoroughly until smooth. If the dip is too thick, add one tablespoon of lemon juice or water and try again. Continue to add on tablespoon at a time, until hummus is smooth. When the cauliflower is done, remove from the oven and serve on a platter or enjoy in a bowl.

Dinner: Chicken and Quinoa Soup

Baked or stir-fried chicken from a previous meal makes an excellent ingredient for this soup. Quinoa is combined with a handful of vegetables and broth to create a satisfying dish, which is perfect from leftovers of a roast dinner, or fresh, raw vegetables can be used.

- 2 cups of cooked chicken (baked or stir-fried)

- 4 cups of broth (chicken or vegetable)

- ½ teaspoon of sea salt

- 1 cup of quinoa (uncooked)

- 1 celery stalk, sliced

- 1 carrot stick, sliced

- Dash of sage

- ½ teaspoon of thyme

- 1 teaspoon of tarragon

Add the four cups of broth to a large cooking pot to boil. Add in the quinoa, as this will take the longest to cook, and reduce to medium. Cook for 10-12 minutes on medium heat with a cover. Add in the chicken, vegetables, and spices. Simmer for another 18-25 minutes or until tender. Serve with fresh rolls or rye bread.

Chapter 6: Best Mindset to Permanent Change your Diet and Your Health

Making positive Changes to Your Lifestyle to Encourage Healthier Eating

How can you switch to better eating habits? It's generally a mindset that helps you focus on your choices and their impact on your health, rather than making impulsive decisions that can lead to bad choices. There are a number of changes you can make, starting today, to help you focus on eating and living well:

- Before you decide to eat a chosen food, ask yourself about the outcome and impact the decision will be. Is it an apple that can be readily enjoyed and give your body the nutrients it needs, or is it a processed snack, such as a candy bar or chocolate, without any value? Always consider the advantage and the outcome of each food, both the short-term and long-term effects.

Exercise, Meditation and a Positive Mindset

Maintaining a positive outlook in life is vital to achieving good health, both physically and mentally. This can be difficult at times, especially when we experience challenges and setbacks. It's normal to feel discouraged and negative when positive changes don't yield results quickly, or we find adapting to new ways more difficult than expected. There are small activities and habits we can implement in our life, to feel a sense of satisfaction and help following a consistent path of a positive outcome:

- Keep a journal of your progress, and note any ideas, new foods, or recipes you want to try. If you feel inspired in any, write it down. An idea or suggestion you write down today can help you at sone point in the future when you feel discouraged.

- Consider that the small changes you make today will result in better decisions and habits for tomorrow.

- Don't be afraid to try new foods with stronger nutritional value, and include them in your diet.

Chapter 7: Mistakes to Avoid and Tips to Get the Best From Healthy Meal Prep Diet Plan

Tips for Making Healthy Eating Easy

As you begin your new path of eating well and making better decisions about the foods you eat, there are some additional tips and suggestions for making the transition easier from a traditional diet to a more health-conscious plan:

- ***Don't always believe everything you read on labels.*** Some brands and products are more accurate than others. There are certain terms that can mislead of cause a misrepresentation of the product; by convincing the customer, it is more natural and healthier than it is. For example, dried fruits are healthy when prepared naturally (sun-dried), though many varieties are chemically treated and not as beneficial as they claim. Salted and flavored nuts and similar threats may be labeled as high in protein and nutrients, though the high levels of sodium and other additives counter the positive effect on any nutrients they contain. To be certain, you choose foods without the risk of harmful ingredients, choose raw and without additional ingredients as much as possible.

- **Drink plenty of water.** Often, we feel hungry when we're dehydrated. Drinking water frequently will avoid the sensation of false hunger and provide a benefit to healthy eating and dieting. Most people do not drink enough water, which can contribute to weight gain and substituting water for soda and other unhealthy beverages. To keep hydrated, carry a reusable bottle and refill it often. Always keep your bottle full and ready to drink whenever you feel slightly hungry, and you'll notice the difference it makes. Water contains minerals that are important for the development and health of our bones and muscles.

- **Read the nutrient contents on each package.** When you choose to buy a packaged food item, carefully review the list of nutrients, and note the amount of nutritional value versus the sugar and carbohydrate content. In some cases, the amount of unhealthy ingredients is exponentially higher than all the nutrients combined, making the choice of buying the food item a waste. If you are not accustomed to reading nutrient lists, it may take some time to become familiar with them. You'll find them resourceful, and over time, you'll automatically know which foods to avoid completely as a result.

- ***Don't feel guilty about errors in judgment.*** This can happen when we choose a food that we mistakenly think is healthy or beneficial for our diet, only to discover it's the exact opposite. In the case of boxed cereals or "real fruit" snacks, always be mindful of how these products are packaged and the nutrient lists. Sometimes, labels such as "no added sugar" or "organic" may convince us that the foods are acceptable, when they have little or no benefit at all. When this happens, consider it a learning process, and be prepared to make mistakes. Food companies know how to market their products in such a way that we are easily convinced there are benefits, even when there are none. Research and experience, over time, are the best methods of defense against making misjudgments in the future.

- **Stay Regularly active.** Exercising regularly will support your new way of healthy eating by helping you avoid chronic health problems associated with bad nutrition and lack of exercise. Keeping fit will prompt us to make better choices in the foods we eat so that we can support the development of muscle tone and a leaner, stronger physique.

Frequently Asked Questions

Question: Should I eat three meals a day, or can I increase or decrease the frequency?

Answer: Three meals a day is a standard or traditional way of eating that most people, even today, still adhere to. There have been studies on both the decreasing of meal frequency, such as intermittent fasting and the dividing of meals into smaller portions for five or six times each day. Overall, there are variations in the findings, and while some people benefit from eating less frequently, others claim the exact opposite. In general, the number of meals you eat depends on your lifestyle and how often you need to "re-fuel" or recharge yourself. For example, people who are extremely active may need more food, and choose to eat smaller, protein and energy-packed mini-meals, such as smoothies, lean meats, and salads, to keep up with their body's demands. For others, eating less often is satisfying enough, as they get the nutrients and energy levels, they need out of fewer meals each day.

Question: *Is it possible to become addicted to unhealthy, junk food, and how can you quit?*

Answer: Yes, junk food high in sugar and sodium can become habit-forming and challenging to quit in exchange for healthier options. The best way to approach switching from unhealthy foods and drinks to better options is to focus on trying new options, and slowly replacing current foods in your diet with newer, more nutrient-rich options. For example, if you drink soda regularly, you may be tempted to switch to diet soda, which is problematic in its lack of nutrition and adverse effects from the unnatural sweeteners. Substituting soda with sparkling water or freshly squeezed juices can be a great way to reduce the level of sugar in your diet. Tackle each negative food item in your diet individually, one at a time, so that you can concentrate on making small, but significant improvements towards your long-term goal.

Question: I'm not seeing results after the three-week meal plan but would like to continue on this diet. How soon will I notice weight loss and other benefits?

Answer: It's important to understand that while most people will see some benefits within the first two or three weeks, this is not consistent for everyone. Everyone has a different body type, metabolism, and other characteristics that are impacted uniquely during a change in diet. In some cases, there are people who may experience negative side effects from a change towards healthier eating, due to the sudden shift from processed foods to better options. This is only temporary and will not last past two weeks. Weight gain is uncommon, though it may occur on rare occasions. Overall, the goal is to adapt to and continue a new, healthier way of eating for the long-term benefits that will improve your health for the rest of your life. Focusing on short-term benefits, while encouraging when they materialize, can be distracting from the life-long goals.

Question: Which is a better option: low carb diet or vegan, plant-based eating?

Answer: Both diets have numerous benefits and will promote weight loss and a healthy lifestyle. Plant-based eating is the preferred meal plan of vegans because all animal-based foods and products are completely avoided, and all nutrients are sourced from vegetables, fruits, grains, nuts, seeds, and soy. While the low carb diet is also a healthy option, some people will continue to add processed food options, simply because they are listed as having low levels of carbohydrates. Low carb or ketogenic eating is beneficial in many ways, due to the focus on healthy fats and moderate protein, though close attention should be paid to choosing quality sources of proteins, unlike some low carb meal plans, which suggest bacon and regular servings of fried foods. Most people who are serious about weight loss and good health will adapt the low carb meal plan to include only good sources of fat, such as fish, avocado, and coconut oil.

There is a third option, which is to combine both vegan and low carb eating together, which requires a lot of research and planning. This is a rewarding way of eating due to the advantages of both diets together. For some people, choosing one or both of these diets can be an ideal way of life, while it doesn't necessarily work for everyone. The key idea is to maintain a diet full of balanced meals, whole foods, and lots of nutrients.

Question: Is it recommended to extend the first week of the meal plan (vegan and vegetarian recipes) into two or three weeks?

Answer: This is an option that is available to you if you find that the benefits of eating all or mostly plant-based foods are showing some advantages early in your diet. You may also find this way of eating suits your own lifestyle, and that eliminating meat altogether maybe your future diet. This can be extended and adapted into low carb eating as well, though this isn't necessary. The three-week meal prep plan is a sample or starter into your new way of eating and will help you determine the future choices you will make for meal preparation.

Question: *Is it dangerous to eat fish too often? What are the risks?*

Answer: Generally, fish is healthy and can be enjoyed on a regular basis, as part of a well-balanced meal plan. Unfortunately, some types of fish or sources where they are from can be contaminated or have a negative impact on the quality of the meat. For example, some people avoid fish harvested from farm fishing, due to concerns about the conditions. Some varieties of fish, such as tuna, have seen an increase in mercury and other contaminants. While there is a valid concern about the accumulation of contaminants in fish and food in general, ocean-caught fish are generally safe. It's also beneficial to research various regions around the world to determine which sources are the best or least contaminated.

Conclusion

Healthy meal preparation is not just about eating well; it's about living a life that supports a good diet, healthy habits, and knowing how to make good decisions about your well being. With the right frame of mind, we can avoid making the mistake of choosing the wrong foods and options, and these changes make an impact on the people in our lives, which may encourage them to adapt some of our new ways of eating and preparation of meals. A balanced way of eating is important for the way we live and share our meals with others. It's an excellent way to explore the many options of food, both globally and locally, we have access to for a well-balanced diet.

9 781802 347951